BEST LITTLE
B👁👁K
OF BIRDS

Timber Press
Workman Publishing
Hachette Book Group, Inc.
1290 Avenue of the Americas
New York, New York 10104
timberpress.com

Timber Press is an imprint of Workman Publishing, a
division of Hachette Book Group, Inc. The Timber Press
name and logo are registered trademarks of Hachette Book
Group, Inc.

Printed in Dongguan, China, (TLF) on
responsibly sourced paper

Jacket design by Vincent James. Text design by Will Brown
based on series design by Vincent James

The publisher is not responsible for websites (or
their content) that are not owned by the publisher.

ISBN 978-1-64326-408-0
A catalog record for this book is available
from the Library of Congress.

BIRDS *of* WASHINGTON & OREGON

The East Side

Tamara Enz

Photography by Greg Smith

TIMBER PRESS

PORTLAND, OREGON

To Bob and Kathie Enz,
with gratitude for
instilling wild in me

CONTENTS

Preface

So often paired together, Washington and Oregon are vastly different places despite their proximity. The Snake and Columbia Rivers slicing through central Washington provide an abundance of water and agricultural opportunity only dreamed of in eastern Oregon, where the Snake and Owyhee Rivers skirt the edges. What they share is expansive geography with a small population offering a place to while away time in pursuit of the rich birdlife that graces the region.

From the continent's greatest river to the tiniest mountain stream, saline lakes to alpine lakes, from roadside habitat among wheat fields to miles of open-range sagebrush, there are birds throughout it all. The more we know about them, the more we appreciate them, the more enriched we are, and the more likely we are to protect the landscape they depend on.

The goal of this book is to introduce more people to these unimaginably adaptable dinosaurs. Yes, dinosaurs. Birds have survived through millions of years of global upheaval, ice ages, shifting continents, rising and falling sea levels, supervolcanoes, and mass extinctions. Yet, they are now facing the most dangerous time, the one in which humans sprawl across the land, climate change eats up shorelines and mountaintop habitat, and unprecedented seasonal fluctuations displace prey. Individually, we may feel unable to change this, but collectively, we make a difference. It behooves us to do everything we can to provide a respite for the birds and accept every chance to help. That is within our power, and the birds will thank us by plying the skies for many millennia to come.

Birding the East Side

I t's a little-known fact that Washington and Oregon have an east side. The western urban areas and the Pacific Coast get most of the fame and glory. The reality is that two-thirds of Oregon and about half of Washington lie east of the Cascade Mountains. In the Cascades, rain shadow, the drier eastern slope drops into sparsely populated high desert, sagebrush steppe and shrublands, grasslands, and ponderosa pine forests. Laced with big rivers and small towns, wildlife refuges, and painted hills, there is an array of habitats and species to pique your interest and offer a lifetime of exploration.

The vast East Side holds four ecoregions that broadly define the scope of this book. The East Cascades run north–south along the narrow eastern front of the Cascades Range, crossing the Columbia River and connecting Washington and Oregon, and continuing south to the California border. The extensive wetlands around Klamath Falls are the only portion of the East Cascades ecoregion included in this book. The Columbia Plateau nestles within the eastern curve of the Columbia River where it splits Washington State. Lying south of the Spokane River in northeastern Washington and north of the Ochoco Mountains (the Blue Mountain ecoregion divide) in Oregon, most of the ecoregion is in Washington and holds the agricultural center, primarily wheat and vineyards in the drylands, and orchards along the rivers. In contrast, the Blue Mountain ecoregion is the largest in Oregon but fills only the far southeastern corner of Washington. Although named for the mountains, the ecoregion is highly diverse, spanning a series of mountain ranges, canyons, and river valleys from the Idaho border to central Oregon. This is where cattle country begins. Rounding out the ecoregions, the Northern Basin and Range of southeast Oregon includes the sagebrush sea, numerous playas, and Steens Mountain, the largest fault-block mountain in North America. A fifth ecoregion, the heavily forested Northern Rockies, in the far northeastern corner of Washington, is not included.

Eastern Washington and Oregon manage to balance the contradiction of being desert and having tremendous water resources. The rivers— the Spokane, Columbia, Snake, Palouse, Tucannon, Walla Walla, Deschutes, Crooked, John Day, Umatilla, Imnaha, Powder, Grand Ronde, Chewaucan, Owyhee—and their canyons are the lifeblood of the region. In addition to the rivers, numerous inland lakes dot the landscape, some natural, some human made, some saline and ephemeral, all unexpected— Potholes, Soap, Moses, Sprague, Summer, Silver, Abert, Hart, Crump, Antelope, Haystack, Wallowa, Borax, Goose—and a veritable wealth of water. Finally, extensive wetlands are harbored in state and federal wildlife refuges and management areas across both states, providing some of the finest migratory layovers anywhere in the world—Umatilla,

Turnbull, Saddle Mountain, McNary, Hanford, Columbia, Toppenish, McKay Creek, Malheur, Upper Klamath.

From the wetlands of tiny Sprague Lake, where Black Terns breed, to the aspen stands of massive Steens Mountain, where Black Rosy-Finches live, 40 state and global Important Bird Areas are found on the East Side. Designated by the National Audubon Society, Important Bird Areas provide essential bird habitat during breeding, wintering, and migration. They also offer opportunities for birders to enjoy the species of the season, with concentrations of birds not commonly found at other times.

On top of this diversity, much of the land is publicly owned and accessible. Along with state parks and wildlife management areas, the federal lands—Umatilla, Wallowa-Whitman, Ochoco, and Malheur National Forests, Hanford Reach, Hart Mountain National Antelope Refuge, Steens Mountain Wilderness, and the extensive holdings of the Bureau of Land Management—are available to everyone.

The riches of a landscape often seen as desolate and empty will provide near-limitless birding opportunities. Take your time to explore, appreciate, and marvel at the adaptations of birds that call the East Side home. You might find you need another expedition to take it all in. And another. And maybe one more, and . . .

With feathers fluffed, a female Anna's Hummingbird enjoys a bath.

East Side Habitats

Driving through the East Side has led many to ponder if anything ever happens here. While the surface may appear somewhat placid and bleak, the history is anything but. For almost 20 million years, volcanic eruptions flooded eastern Washington and Oregon and parts of Idaho and Nevada with lava. The basalt accumulated to depths of 10,000 feet in some areas, and individual flows have been tracked as far as 100 miles. Over another few million years, this lava bed was tipped up by tectonic activity, and windblown sediments from the west, including ash from the active coastal volcanoes, piled up—to depths of 200 feet—to create the Palouse Prairie.

More time passed, and the last great ice ages set in, seemingly a time of slow motion and steady-state geology. Although the ice mass didn't get much past present-day Spokane, the region bore the brunt of glaciation in a different form. As the ice sheets encroached from the north, they cut off and dammed rivers, flooding vast areas. Occasionally, the ice dams rotted and broke, causing catastrophic floods across eastern Washington; slowly, the ice rebuilt, blocking and flooding again. The most recent and largest lake, Glacial Lake Missoula, formed 18,000 to 20,000 years ago. Stretching 200 miles, Glacial Lake Missoula stood more than 4,000 feet above sea level and was 2,000 feet deep. At the lake's end,

More spunk per ounce than most, this Anna's Hummingbird male turns a fierce eye on the competition.

the glacier's south-reaching finger formed an ice dam on the Clark Fork River of western Montana. When this dam broke, the resulting flood scoured the Columbia Plateau with water raging at a velocity ten times greater than the combined velocity of all current rivers in the world.

This is a greatly simplified version of the region's geologic past, but it identifies the primary influences visible in the landscape: volcanism, glaciation, and flooding. The factors shaping today's habitat and its inhabitants are similar: intensely hot summers and cold winters and the flow of water through the landscape. Within this larger scheme, the East Side holds the four primary terrestrial biomes in the world—alpine, desert, grassland, and forest.

A curious male Lazuli Bunting stretches for a better look.

Rarely caught at rest, Cedar Waxwings settle for the night.

SAGEBRUSH STEPPE AND SHRUBLANDS

Although most people see sagebrush as a crowd of indistinguishable bushes, there are several sagebrush species, and sagebrush density—whether the landscape is grass dense and shrub poor or shrub dense and grass poor—indicates steppe versus shrublands. Whether steppe or shrublands, sagebrush communities grow across a wide range of conditions. The community structure varies with soil, elevation, water availability, and fire and grazing history. Numerous other shrubby plants, like saltbush and Mormon tea (also called ephedra), and smaller shrubs, like rabbitbrush and snakeweed, mix in unnoticed. In relatively healthy sagebrush habitat, an occasional western juniper or mountain mahogany adds structural relief. Joining the shrubs, sagebrush and otherwise, are a variety of grasses and forbs. Sagebrush habitat sometimes fringes wetlands, rivers, and mountain meadows and can be found stretching into ponderosa pine and Douglas fir forests.

The iconic sagebrush bird species are the Sagebrush Sparrow and Sage Thrasher. Also, look for Red-tailed Hawk, American Kestrel, Turkey Vulture, Long-billed Curlew, Say's Phoebe, Horned Lark, Savannah Sparrow, Ash-throated Flycatcher, and Common Nighthawk. Sites to

A Lewis's Woodpecker blushes pink against the sky.

Western Kingbirds frequent barbed wire fences in search of insects.

explore include Moses Coulee and Beezley Hills Preserve; Palouse River Watershed; Saddle and Rattlesnake Mountains; McNary, Umatilla, and McKay Creek National Wildlife Refuges; Thief Valley Reservoir; Oregon Badlands Wilderness; John Day Fossil Beds National Monument; and Steens Mountain.

BIRDING TIPS: The sagebrush comes alive in the cool early morning when small birds sing from their sagebrush perches, and raptors sun themselves on power poles and cliffs. When hiking through dense sagebrush, keep an eye out for rattlesnakes and ground-nesting birds.

CONSERVATION CONCERNS: Sagebrush steppe is threatened by overgrazing, urban sprawl, increased wildfire, invasive plants, and energy development, but the overarching threat exacerbating the other concerns is climate change. State and federal agencies and several conservation organizations are working to reduce fire load and control cheatgrass, an annual invasive that has increased fire intensity, and are conducting restoration to reduce erosion and improve habitat.

A male American Kestrel puffs up against the cold.

Out of context, a Sage Thrasher pauses on an outcrop.

Black-billed Magpies are big birds; glossy and vocal, they are hard to miss.

FOREST

Across most of eastern Washington and Oregon, forest means ponderosa pine. The most widespread forest type in the western United States, ponderosa pine is versatile. Fitting into many landscapes, elevations, and water regimes, it is heat, cold, and drought tolerant. As elevation increases, ponderosas are replaced mostly by fir and hemlock before reaching the subalpine and alpine zones. Aspens can be found mixed with conifers at higher elevations in the mountains and as pure stands on Steens Mountain. Most bottomlands have been developed, and remnant riparian forest is found only in small patches. Dominated by cottonwoods, alder, and aspen, with dense understory thickets of willow and dogwood, the vegetation and availability of water make these spots rich in birdlife.

Birds to look for in ponderosa forest are Ruby-crowned Kinglet, Orange-crowned Warbler, Townsend's Solitaire, Steller's Jay, the woodpeckers, chickadees, and nuthatches. Look for Clark's Nutcracker at higher elevation. In the riparian zone, look for Great Horned Owls, Western Wood-Pewee, woodpeckers and sapsuckers, and Yellow-breasted Chat. Forest in most of eastern Washington is limited, but the Blue Mountains in the southeastern corner of the state have an affinity for Rocky Mountain species, including some otherwise not commonly seen; look here for Williamson's Sapsucker, Bohemian Waxwing, Redpoll, and Pine Grosbeak. Sites to explore include Fields Spring, Emigrant Springs, Battle Mountain Forest, and Wallowa Lake State Parks; Unity Lake State Recreation Area; and Steens Mountain.

BIRDING TIPS: When forest birds hide in treetops and river bottom thickets or angle behind tree trunks, being able to identify their calls is a valuable skill. Take advantage of trails, riverbanks, and forest openings that allow better treetop views. Forest types sometimes blend one into the next as you change elevation or move up- or downriver; take the time to explore each community, as they will likely produce different bird species. Spring migration brings waves of passerines, while fall produces a steady stream of birds funneling south. In winter, when many small species forage together in the short daylight hours, birds can be active and noisy, making them easier to track.

CONSERVATION CONCERNS: Timber harvesting and grazing changed the forest, reducing water quality and quantity. A century of fire suppression created heavy fuel loads. Exacerbated by climate change and warmer winters, suppression also created epidemic insect and disease outbreaks that have taken a toll on trees and habitats. After long-term fire suppression, wildfires have become catastrophic. Rather than regular low burns that clear blowdown and brush, they often become canopy fires, killing the fire-adapted trees and burning the understory down to mineral soil. Riparian forests were cut to expand agriculture in the rich bottomlands. Regeneration is limited by development and the changed hydrology of dammed rivers that no longer scour riverbanks or open soils for pioneer species to establish.

Holes up, holes across, a Red-breasted Sapsucker at work.

Looking like a bit of loose bark, Brown Creepers spiral up trees and flutter down to the base of the next.

A male Red-naped Sapsucker sports a red chin and forehead as well.

Yellow-breasted Chats tend to lurk in the shadows; it's rare to catch one out.

WETLANDS

Wetlands occur where the soil is covered or saturated with water for at least part of the year, typically including the growing season. This produces unique habitats because plants require special adaptations to survive in saturated soils. Wetlands can include the sedges, bulrushes, and cattails we commonly see, but can also be cottonwood forests that follow river bottoms and tolerate high water tables and flood scouring. Many of the wetlands on the East Side are shallow basins that collect rainwater and snowmelt. Wetlands provide varied feeding, breeding, and migrating opportunities regardless of a bird's life stage: bare shoreline, shallow or deep water; insects and other invertebrates, plant seeds and roots for food; shelter from predators; nesting and chick-rearing habitat; migratory resting and refueling stops. Despite centuries of dismissal as mere swamps, wetlands are some of the most important and productive habitats on the planet.

Common wetland birds are Black-necked Stilt, American Avocet, sandpipers, Osprey, Common Yellowthroat, Yellow Warbler, Black-headed Grosbeak, and Red-winged, Yellow-headed, and Brewer's Blackbirds. Sites to explore include Potholes State Park; Crab Creek Road Wildlife

Area; Crooked River Wetlands Complex; and Turnbull, McNary, Columbia, Malheur, and Klamath Marsh National Wildlife Refuges.

BIRDING TIPS: Wetlands can be difficult to access; back roads that travel along wetland edges and parks with trails, boardwalks, or decks through wet areas provide the best opportunities to see the inner workings of wetland birdlife. National wildlife refuges often have driving tours and viewing platforms that provide wetland birdwatching opportunities. A scope can be handy in these places.

CONSERVATION CONCERNS: Wetlands continue to be filled for development and agriculture. Dams created ponded water, eliminating wetland edges. Water pollution and toxic buildup from contaminated storm runoff can be problematic if it is beyond the capacity of the wetland to store and filter. Changing precipitation patterns are also of concern.

Active and vocal, Marsh Wrens can be easy to track but hard to see.

Male Common Yellowthroats are known to fight their reflections in nearby windows.

Heard winnowing in the spring, Wilson's Snipes often come to rest on fence posts and stumps.

Bullies of the bog, Yellow-headed Blackbirds arrive late in the spring.

The runway models of the bird world, Black-necked Stilts are all leg.

LAKES, RIVERS, AND RESERVOIRS

Water on the East Side is a fickle thing. Precipitation throughout the region is low, averaging about 12 inches a year, but there is water. The big rivers flow through the desert, bringing water from mountain ranges in surrounding states and Canada and other wetter places upstream. The lakes and reservoirs have perennial water from precipitation, groundwater, snowmelt, and streams. This water and its catchment are what keep the landscape thrumming. Without this resource, above all others, nothing could live here. Some basins are alkaline or saline—Lake Abert, for example. For humans, the usefulness is naught. For migrating birds feasting on the bounty of brine shrimp, this is heaven. If you're looking for life, go where the water is.

You will find the usual open-water suspects here: geese, ducks, grebes, cormorants, pelicans, gulls, and terns. The latter three groups tend to be fair-weather summer visitors, but the remainder are commonly seen year-round. Sites to explore include Riverside and Lyons Ferry State Parks; Wanapum Recreation Area; Potholes Reservoir; McNary National Wildlife Refuge; Bennington and Jubilee Lakes; Quesna County Park; Haystack, Prineville, Beulah, and Antelope Reservoirs; and Silver, Summer, Abert, Hart, and Goose Lakes.

Red-breasted Mergansers would be better named Red-billed or Red-legged Mergansers.

The rufous head and green mask are a giveaway on a male Green-winged Teal.

BIRDING TIPS: The best time to find ducks and shorebirds is during migration. Marsh birds like blackbirds and wrens are most active and raucous in the spring and on early summer mornings. Rather than standing, sit down to scan open water to avoid spooking birds. It is easier to maintain a safe distance with a scope. Always obey signs indicating closed areas and keep dogs leashed. Humans and off-leash dogs disrupt feeding shorebirds and can interfere with ground-nesting birds.

CONSERVATION CONCERNS: Pollution and excessive erosion from land-use changes and agriculture, road runoff, and wastewater are ongoing issues. Many East Side rivers are dammed, creating stagnant backwater and heavy silt loads. These waters can be bird-friendly for diving ducks, but are often too warm and slow for the salmon that once thrived here. Overcommitted water allotments, excessive irrigation, and illegal dams and water draws are also concerns. Reservoirs change the landscape by flooding previously dry sites, drowning wetland fringes and uplands. In addition, hydrology is altered by limiting downstream flow and decreasing sediment load below dams. Tourism and recreation can also be problematic when desert lakes, rivers, and reservoirs are loved to death.

PRAIRIE AND GRASSLAND

Once covering 18,000 square miles of the inland Pacific Northwest in Washington, Oregon, and Idaho, the Palouse Prairie held deep, old soils and received high rainfall (15 to 30 inches per year), producing lush bunchgrasses, fescues, and junegrass interspersed with forbs, and low shrubs like snowberry and wild rose. These rolling hills have been almost entirely converted to agriculture, reducing the prairie to a fraction of its original area and making it one of the continent's most endangered habitats. Plowing the soils changed the hydrology, increasing the speed and quantity of runoff and erosion, and reducing groundwater recharge. Stream cutting deepened, resulting in drier land less able to support dense grasses. Farther west on the Columbia Plateau, there were low-elevation grasslands along river bottoms and semidesert grasslands (5 to 10 inches of precipitation a year, typically in winter) at mid-elevations. These areas have also been almost entirely converted to agriculture. Dominated by bunchgrasses like needle and thread, three awn, and dropseed, these grasslands had scattered shrubs and filled the arid landscape between the big rivers. At higher elevations, grasslands are sometimes found in the alpine and subalpine zones and on mountain balds.

Grasslands don't always appear lively, but take the time to watch and listen—there is a lot of life hidden here. Look for Savannah Sparrows and other ground-nesting birds clinging to bunchgrasses and forbs or low perches. Lazuli Buntings flit along the edges of shrubby draws, and

Look for Long-billed Curlews in open grasslands and spring fallow fields.

Bewick's Wrens sometimes impersonate Rock Wrens.

hummingbirds refuel on prairie flowers. Raptors, especially Northern Harriers, dip their wings over swales, and Prairie Falcons zoom by in full-speed flight. Ducks and wading birds gather on prairie ponds. Sandhill Cranes hunt in wet meadows, and swallows and swifts weave through the skies above the water and grasses. The premier site to explore is Zumwalt Prairie, a Nature Conservancy property outside Joseph, Oregon. There are remnant prairie patches in Kamiak Butte County Park, Steptoe Butte State Park, and Hells Canyon. Grassland patches can also be found on slopes too steep to plow and on the west-facing foothills of the Blue Mountains above Walla Walla and Milton-Freewater.

BIRDING TIPS: In areas with more topography, search the draws for species more prone to brushy areas and look for perching raptors blending into the branches of chokecherries and hawthorns. Ground lovers like Horned Larks and Mourning Doves often congregate in two-tracks and trails. Watch overhead for Swainson's Hawks in summer and Red-tailed and Rough-legged Hawks in winter. Fences and power poles commonly hold bluebirds, shrikes, and American Kestrels.

CONSERVATION CONCERNS: Development and conversion to agriculture are ongoing threats; invasive plants, especially annual grasses including cheatgrass, diminish prairie area and quality and increase fire risk and damage; chemical pesticides, herbicides, and fertilizers pollute rivers and can have lethal and sublethal effects on birds and many other species. Reintroducing restorative fire to prairies is difficult in the dry West.

The graceful female Barn Swallow caught at a bad time.

Wild Turkeys typically move in packs.

CLIFFS, CANYONS, AND TALUS

Often we look at rock with no thought beyond it being hard and uninteresting, but rock on the East Side takes on new proportions. Cliff height and canyon depth are inspiring and offer perspective. Talus fields demand a level of dexterity and ambition beyond most of us. Rock formation and destruction, volcanic eruptions, glaciation and glacial floods, and the everyday wear and tear of water, wind, and life moving over rock for millions of years—the geological forces and time required to create this landscape are beyond most people's scale of understanding. What we often see as just more wasteland in a desert full of wasteland is actually rife with life; insects, reptiles, amphibians, birds, mammals, and plants take advantage of every shelf, niche, and hole in the rocks.

Look for Peregrine Falcons, Ferruginous Hawks, Golden Eagles, Violet-green and Cliff Swallows, Rock and Canyon Wrens, Great Horned Owls, and Common Ravens. The canyon walls and river bottoms of the Grande Ronde River and Wawawai Canyons, and the Cottonwood, John Day,

The opening to a Cliff Swallow nest is often just large enough for entry.

Magicians with mud, Cliff Swallows build gravity-defying homes.

and Owyhee Canyons hold an array of habitats and associated species and are spectacular places to explore. Scan the steep east face of Steens Mountain and the west face of Hart Mountain for cliff-nesting raptors. Catlow Valley Road follows the west-facing Catlow Rim and offers numerous places to stop and scan, and driving to the top of Steens Mountain offers a rare view from the rim.

BIRDING TIPS: Loose rock, steep walls, and intense heat are possible hazards. Know your limitations, and don't push beyond what is reasonable to tackle with your skills. This remote area offers little recourse if you're tangled up in a rockslide or fall off a cliff face. Be aware of the slope, trail conditions, and footing. Do not disturb nesting raptors; a scope is a nice way to enjoy the view without hiking in uncertain terrain or disrupting the birds.

CONSERVATION CONCERNS: Rock mining, cliff-edge encroachment by development, and raptor nest disturbance are the primary concerns.

Vivid color and agile flight define Tree Swallows.

ALPINE

In eastern Washington and Oregon, the alpine zone begins at roughly 9,000 feet. Climbing above subalpine fir and whitebark pine interspersed with high mountain meadows of fescues and sedges, you top out in sparse whitebark pine communities. These high places tend toward bare rock, talus, and scattered grasses and wildflowers, deep snows linger into summer, and utterly clear alpine lakes offer respite from a long hike.

Birds to look for include Clark's Nutcracker, Pine Siskin, Common Raven, Hermit Thrush, Mountain Bluebird, and Golden Eagle. Alpine zones are restricted to the high elevations of the Wallowa, Strawberry, and Elkhorn Mountains and Steens Mountain.

BIRDING TIPS: Hiking in the mountains of eastern Washington and Oregon can be rewarding for so many reasons. If you are in pursuit of a few high-elevation birds, all the better. Be prepared for elevation gains and changing weather, wear good hiking boots, and carry food and water. Starting from Frenchglen and Page Springs Campground, the loop road on Steens Mountain goes almost to the rim, making the alpine zone accessible. Steens is anomalous because the vegetation

Clark's Nutcracker calls are often heard echoing off cliff faces in the high country.

An immature male Mountain Bluebird hasn't quite reached full vibrancy.

moves from juniper to sagebrush and aspens but has no fir or pine forest. It also tops out at a cliff overlooking the Alvord Desert. Because of this, it offers different species, like Golden Eagles, at the rim. Completing the tour loop is not recommended as the road is unkept; better to return to Frenchglen the way you entered. Wild horses, the Kiger mustangs, descendants of feral Spanish horses from the seventeenth century, roam freely in the sagebrush of Steens Mountain.

CONSERVATION CONCERNS: Climate change is the big driver in the loss of alpine habitat. Animals can move north, and some plant communities can move up in elevation, but there are no corridors for alpine plants to travel north, and there is no up if you are already in the alpine zone. This behooves us to be especially mindful of our behavior when birding at elevation. Stay on the trails, pack out all trash, be careful with fire, keep dogs on leash, and make sure gear is clean before hiking to prevent spreading invasive species.

AGRICULTURE

Much of the East Side, the rolling eastern prairies, and the sagebrush steppe have been converted to agriculture. Vineyards, orchards, wheat fields, feedlots, alfalfa, and open range have changed its face. Still, among this, many species have found a place to call home. Fencerows, unplowed draws, and shelter belts offer habitat to smaller birds, and farm buildings attract insectivores and granivores, as well as those looking for a rodent lunch. The open agricultural lands provide late fall and winter habitat for birds that use open ground, feed on waste grain, or feed on birds that feed on waste grain. Raptors soar above all.

BIRDING TIPS: Horned Larks, sparrows, and meadowlarks are common in mixed agricultural land, and Long-billed Curlews sometimes are found in the stubble of old wheat fields. Small ponds scattered throughout the plateau often host a handful of ducks and wading birds. Look for raptors on power poles, riding the thermals above open fields, and perched on cliffs and bluffs surrounding them. Swallows, pigeons, doves, and House Sparrows are likely near buildings. Pay attention to private land and "No Trespassing" signs. A scope may be helpful for ponds not near the road. Sites to explore include the wheat fields between Wasco and Cottonwood Canyon State Park. After scanning the roadsides, drop into the canyon to see its birdlife. Milton-Freewater to Pilot Rock offers dozens of back roads and side canyons to explore. Most of eastern Washington, whether Columbia Plateau or Palouse Prairie, is navigable along township and range lines delineating the farmland. The rolling topography and landscape texture provide limitless opportunities to find birds.

CONSERVATION CONCERNS: The next step in the conversion progression of prairies and plateaus to agriculture is from agriculture to pavement and development. Losing land that provides both humans and birds with food is a double tragedy.

More often seen on gravel and sand, a Killdeer cools its feet.

Unmistakable male Ring-necked Pheasants have red fleshy cheeks and eyebrows.

Conservation Issues

Sensitive species, red/yellow/orange list, watch list, threatened, endangered, monitored, candidate, common bird in steep decline—these are state, federal, Audubon, American Birding Association (ABA), and Partners in Flight designations for 25 percent (51 of 207) of the bird species included in this book. Some species carry multiple warnings; Long-billed Curlews, for instance, are on the ABA/Audubon yellow list, are monitored in Washington, and are a sensitive species in Oregon. The International Union for Conservation of Nature and Natural Resources (IUCN) reports that 12 percent of the bird species they have assessed globally are threatened with extinction—given the current listings and concerns for the East Side species, we are running at twice that rate.

Sagebrush steppe was once the dominant vegetative community of eastern Washington. Covering 12 million acres and a third of the state, land-use conversion and fragmentation have reduced it to about 4 million remaining acres. The largest intact tracts, comprising 2 million acres, are the Hanford Site and the Yakima Training Center and are subject to destruction of a different form. In Oregon, the list of sagebrush habitat

Often hunting from a perch, Prairie Falcons are fast and direct when on the wing.

A Great Egret reflects on the hue of early morning.

assaults runs like a rap sheet: 82 percent in the Blue Mountains lost, 87 percent on the Columbia Plateau gone, 59 percent destroyed in the Northern Basin and Range. Additionally, grasslands are one of the most imperiled habitats in the West and continue to decline in Washington and Oregon.

Conversion to agriculture and residential development have taken the greatest toll. Add habitat loss and fragmentation from energy development, roads, and transmission and power lines. Don't forget to include livestock grazing, invasive species, erosion, and increased fire intensity and frequency on the list of pressing issues. Top it off with climate change—changing temperatures, too much rain, not enough rain, rain at the wrong time; changes in habitat structure resulting from climate change; insect hatches and ripening seed and fruit now out of sync with chick-rearing. These are the cumulative impacts birds must endure to continue their cycles of breeding and migrating.

The good news is that human populations remain low on the East Side, and while development and sprawl are happening, much of the land is still concrete- and asphalt-free. It is easier to conserve and restore land that doesn't come with a complement of pavement and where precipitation can soak into the ground, supporting the plants and animals and water table naturally. Additionally, there are vast expanses of public lands and many of them hold extensive wetland systems that support migratory populations beyond imagination.

What can we do as individuals to support birds in this landscape? Work with your state agency representatives, local parks, and conservation organizations to understand the issues birds face. Volunteer to remove invasive species, replant riparian habitats, help stabilize streambanks, build beaver dam analogs—or better yet, restore beavers. Work with farmers and ranchers to increase irrigation efficiency, decrease fertilizer runoff, increase awareness about water pollution from lawns and roadways, manage grazing, limit livestock access to riverbanks, and encourage providing water for livestock away from riparian areas. Encourage the agencies to limit off-road vehicle use on public lands and to close roads wherever possible. Support work to reduce fuel load in forests and strive to reintroduce natural fire and hydrologic regimes. Opportunities for conservation and restoration abound. See the list of birding and conservation organizations in the Recommended Resources section at the end of this book for a place to start.

Streamlined for flying and diving, a Belted Kingfisher wings by.

Pesticides

Fifty years after DDT was banned for unintended environmental consequences, including precipitous population declines in several raptor species, an estimated 1 billion pounds of pesticides are still used in the United States annually—20 percent of global use. Neonicotinoids, the most-used class of pesticides and accounting for more than $3 billion of sales and 25 percent of pesticides used globally, are a systemic insect neurotoxin commonly used to coat commercial agricultural seed—corn, soy, and wheat—and seed for residential lawns and gardens. However, these insecticides are indiscriminate and affect more than the intended target. Highly water-soluble, neonicotinoids leach into soil and surface water, affecting downstream aquatic insects and the many birds and animals that feed on them. Use of these chemicals has been implicated in the widespread decline of insects and, subsequently, the decline of insectivorous birds. Additionally, birds gleaning treated seed show impacts on their metabolic and reproductive systems, orientation, and ability to initiate migration, reducing their overall fitness and chance of survival. The toxins become more concentrated as they move up the food chain into raptors and scavengers, damaging species well beyond the field or yard where the pesticide was initially applied.

If we spoke Barn Swallow, we would hear "Ban neonicotinoids!"

How to Help Birds

PICK UP plastic and other trash when hiking or birding.

RESPECT signed nesting areas.

AVOID disturbing nesting and migrating birds.

MAINTAIN a safe distance from birds, and leash your dog.

DECREASE fuel and energy use.

REDUCE water use and pollution.

MONITOR chemical use in your home and garden, and properly dispose of waste.

VOLUNTEER for a conservation or restoration project.

ADVOCATE for your favorite bird and environmental issues.

Gear and Safety

One of the beauties of birdwatching is that, at its most fundamental, you need nothing more than your eyes and ears. Of course, binoculars or a spotting scope can contribute to the experience, but some of the best birding memories happen without these. That said, 8x or 10x magnification binoculars are worth carrying. Buy the best binoculars you can afford. The more you bird, the more you will appreciate the clarity that good optics provide. A spotting scope, 20x–60x magnification, is useful when birding in grassland or sagebrush. Waterproof optics are always valuable, even in mostly dry places. A camera or smartphone is useful for capturing rare birds and helping with identification challenges. Smartphone apps for visual and auditory identification assistance are invaluable additions to any birder's resources. The most basic gear includes suitable clothing for the conditions; weather can change quickly and dramatically depending on the elevation and habitat. Cool mornings can turn into hot days, and hot days can quickly turn into cold nights. Being prepared can mean the difference between enjoying a day of birding and being cold and wet or overheated and dehydrated.

One of the great attractions of the East Side is the sparse population and remote wildness. This brings a different level of necessary preparation. Be aware of the weather; rain and snow can turn back roads into ball-bearing gumbo. Conversely, summer heat and low rainfall create washboards that rattle your teeth and your vehicle's suspension. Don't park on the shoulder of muddy roads where you can sink up to the axle or over dry vegetation that can be easily ignited by a hot engine. Pack a shovel for both possibilities and extra water to help thwart a fire or cool your engine if necessary. Carry a jack and spare tire, not a donut—there may not be a garage to repair a flat for well over the maximum distance a donut can travel. Speaking of donuts, along with basic vehicle gear and appropriate clothing, take extra food and drinking water.

Always be aware of your surroundings, your footing, and potential hazards. Wear good boots and long pants against spiky desert plants. Keep in mind that rattlesnakes enliven this landscape and don't always announce themselves. They want nothing more than to stay away from you, but they move slowly in cool temperatures and may not have the energy to get out of your way. It's better to sidestep them and let them go undisturbed.

Accessibility

Birds are indiscriminate and make themselves available to everyone. Fortunately, both Washington and Oregon have parks that can accommodate birders with mobility challenges. The Washington State Parks website (parks.wa.gov/find-activity/activity-search/ada-accessible-recreation) includes an interactive map with information on accommodations of interest. The Oregon State Parks website map (stateparks.oregon.gov/index.cfm?do=visit.find#) can be searched using ADA facilities as a feature, and the Oregon State website has an online guide called *Oregon Accessibility Travel Guide* (oregon.gov/oprd/AO/Documents/ACCESS-accessibililty-travel-guide.pdf) that covers accessible public lands and adaptive outfitters. Birdability.org offers a crowd-sourced interactive accessibility map for birding sites around the world. Additionally, anyone can submit information to continue building this inclusive map. At the end of this book is a list of accessible birding sites.

Birding Ethics

The priority of every birder is the health and safety of the birds. Respect the fact that you are in their habitat and create as little disturbance as possible. Heed bird behavior. If birds become agitated or show indications of stress, retreat immediately. Be mindful not to cause disruption at nesting sites or migratory feeding and resting locations. Leash your dog.

While birding apps make identifying birds by sound a snap, be aware that playback of birdsong can cause distress among the local birds. If you must play a recording, use earbuds, or listen in a closed vehicle.

Be responsible and polite to other people and their property. Don't trespass; do respect areas closed to the public. The American Birding Association Code of Ethics can be found here: aba.org/aba-code-of-birding-ethics/.

The East Side supports a remarkable diversity of shorebirds, including this Semipalmated Plover.

A Trumpeter Swan and its cygnet glide through a marsh.

Bird Names for Birds

Birds are named for a variety of factors, including plumage, geographical range, and song. In the past, species were sometimes named for the European or American who first scientifically identified the species or was present during the expedition that first recorded it; Lewis's Woodpecker and Vaux's Swift are examples of this. Moving birders into the twenty-first century means maintaining a progressive attitude toward the activity and, beyond its impact on birds, its impact on society. While no bird will speak out against the name imposed on it, we can. Continuing to honor those who represent the colonial and exploitative past via common bird names implies, at best, indifference toward those who were, and continue to be, harmed by that past. In 2023, the American Ornithological Society, the official arbiter of common bird

The Cornell Lab of Ornithology website eBird.org is the ultimate citizen science project. Free and available to all users globally, data are compiled to assess, for instance, species distribution, abundance, and habitat use. Users of the website and app, which is available offline, can track their personal birding trips and lists, view real-time species distributions, find birding hotspots, and receive alerts for rare bird sightings, all while contributing to the broader data set.

names, announced that they will rename all species identified with people and with otherwise offensive common names. Initially renaming 70 to 80 species occurring in the United States and Canada, they will also revise the naming process. As evolving humans, providing a safe birding experience, free of biases and open to all, is a step toward a more inclusive future.

Lewis's Woodpecker may soon have a new name.

Girls Only

A common bias in birding is the ubiquitous practice of identifying the males while dismissing the females as too much the same, not bright and beautiful enough, or too challenging. Birds in winter plumage and some of the less conspicuous species can also fall prey to this discrimination. Without consciously focusing on female (and other sometimes nondescript) birds, we lose the opportunity to close knowledge gaps about habitat differences and needs, how climate change may affect females during incubation, what both sexes need for reproductive success and, ultimately, species survival. Learn more about Female Bird Day and the Galbatross Project at femalebirdday.wordpress.com.

A female Western Bluebird
sparkles with raindrops.

Using This Book

All living things that have been scientifically identified have a series of classifications consisting of consecutively smaller, genetically related divisions, from animal, for example, to vertebrate, bird, swan, and Tundra Swan. The last three definitive divisions are family, genus (plural is "genera"), and species. Families and genera are groupings with similar characteristics and behaviors. Species is the final, unique identifier for every living thing, each of which bears a scientific Latin name and a common name. While most field guides present birds in their strict phylogenetic order, birds in this book are grouped differently. For ease of identification, unrelated species sharing similar habitats and habits are grouped together, regardless of official family designation. For example, swifts and swallows, although unrelated, are both aerial insectivores that live on the wing and are therefore presented together.

The 123 species in this book are those most likely to be seen in eastern Oregon and eastern Washington during an average birding day in the right season and habitat. Additionally, 84 potentially confusing similar species are included.

The following information is provided for each species:

PHOTOS
of each species, male and female, when different, and seasonal variations when appropriate

CAPTIONS
note significant characteristics to aid identification.

HABITAT AND BEHAVIOR Suitable ecosystems and anticipated habitats are provided. Behaviors include foraging strategies, foods taken, breeding habits, and other pertinent information to distinguish the species.

YEARLY ABUNDANCE Birds have loose schedules that we can track and are often habitat-specific through the seasons. While there are no guarantees, combining this information provides an estimated possibility of seeing a given species, identified here as Rare, Uncommon, Common, or Very Common.

> **RARE** Seeing this bird would be a special event not soon forgotten.
> **UNCOMMON** These birds may require habitat-specific searches or carefully scheduled birding trips to catch them in the right place at the right time.
> **COMMON** Readily seen many days in many places, these are the bread-and-butter birds that make every trip worthwhile.
> **VERY COMMON** These birds are ubiquitous, seen most days in many places.

Additionally, the listed locations (generally presented zigzagging from the northeast near Spokane to the southwest at Klamath) provide a starting point for exploration. Whether you are a new birder becoming familiar with habitat and species or a traveler discovering the East Side for the first time, these suggestions will get you started. Some locations are gleaned from eBird (ebird.org); beware that their names may not readily match your map. The following abbreviations are used:

CA conservation area
CP county park
HMU habitat management unit
NF national forest
NM national monument
NWR national wildlife refuge
RA recreation area
SP state park
WA wildlife area
WMA wildlife management area
WRA wildlife recreation area

SOUNDS Birds declare territory, attract mates, chase predators, and warn others of danger with their songs and calls. To humans, bird sounds are subjective and not easily translated into written form. Descriptions given here are the best transliteration or sensory estimation of bird songs and calls for species in this region.

SIMILAR BIRDS Many bird species look alike and require care to discern. Information about how to distinguish between species is found here. Some similar species have independent accounts; other less common birds may have a photo in their doppelganger's account.

SIZE OF THE BIRD in length (head to tail) and wingspan.

Bird Family Descriptions

Each bird in this book belongs to a genus and a family. Some genera and families are small, like those of the Osprey. Others are the equivalent of extended families with dozens of cousins and once-removed designations, true of the pigeons and doves. Recognizing familial attributes helps simplify potential identification options by eliminating birds that do not fit higher-level characteristics.

GEESE, SWANS & DUCKS (family Anatidae)

Broadly distributed across aquatic habitat types, this family ranges from herbivorous to carnivorous. Larger than ducks, geese often flock and are vociferous. They walk easily but do not dive, and they graze both on land and in shallow water. Ducks are broadly classified as dabbling or diving. Dabblers are commonly found in smaller waterbodies and forage by upending in shallow water. Divers forage in deeper water by fully submerging. Divers can be awkward on land and need extensive open water to take flight, whereas dabblers can take off explosively straight up from the water's surface. Swans are the largest waterfowl. They feed on land and water, and despite their size, they dabble.

COOTS (family Rallidae)

In the same family as the secretive rails, coots are the extroverted cousins. Often seen on open water, they are adept swimmers commonly found in large flocks. Body and bill shape help distinguish coots from ducks. Like grebes, coots have lobed toes that help them swim; unlike grebes, they are also adept at walking in mud and on floating vegetation.

QUAIL (family Odontophoridae)

Restricted to the midlatitudes of the New World and central Africa, these ground-foraging birds are commonly seen in family coveys and various habitats. Busy in the underbrush, scratching for seeds, fruit, and insects, they are in constant motion and often quietly vocal. Seemingly flowing across the landscape, they hop onto obstacles, scale fences, and return to the ground fluidly, flying only when flushed. Adult pairs share nesting and chick-raising duties and stay with the young into the fall.

TURKEYS & PHEASANTS (family Phasianidae)

Notably absent from South America and expectedly from Antarctica, pheasants, grouse, and allies fill most habitats across the remaining globe. Domestic chickens and their eggs are the best-known representatives, appearing daily in a grocery store near you. Mating and breeding are varied affairs, but males are often conspicuous with spectacular plumage and elaborate mating displays. All species nest on the ground; chicks are mobile and begin foraging soon after hatching. Oregon's most iconic species of this family is the Greater Sage-Grouse. A federal species of concern and listed as endangered in Washington, it has been at the center of land-use and development controversy in the West for decades.

GREBES (family Podicipedidae)

Expert diving birds, grebes nest on freshwater and commonly winter in nearshore saltwater. Propelled by powerful legs, their lobed toes provide maneuverability underwater. This does not translate to ease of movement on land, however, and grebes build nests that float or are anchored to shoreline vegetation. Both adults contribute to brood-rearing; chicks often ride on the back of one parent while the other forages. Grebe populations suffer from loss and alteration of habitat, invasive fish species, and human fishing practices.

CORMORANTS (family Phalacrocoracidae)

Cormorants are most readily recognized resting on pilings and rocks with wings outstretched. Expert divers like loons and grebes, cormorants are more land dependent as their feathers are not durably waterproof. Therefore, cormorants perch and hold their wings open to dry; this may also help regulate body temperature. Unlike loons and grebes, cormorants are colonial nesters, and chicks stay in the nest for two to three months before fledging.

PELICANS (family Pelecanidae)

Enormous birds found on coastal and inland waters, pelicans catch fish by plunging headfirst (Brown Pelicans) or schooling fish together and scooping them into their voluminous throat pouches (White Pelicans). Often seen soaring at great heights or taking advantage of ground effect, which buoys birds a fraction of an inch above the water's surface, they commonly move in small flocks. Brown Pelicans nest in marine environments, while White Pelicans are inland creatures; all are colonial nesters.

CRANES (family Gruidae)

Revered through history as bringers of fortune and longevity, the 15 species of this family are elegant. Congregating in vast migratory flocks, they make a raucous, glorious seasonal celebration. Most prefer wet habitats but are found in open spaces on all continents except South America and Antarctica. One of the few nearly monogamous bird species, pairs mate for life. Six species breed in Africa and Australia; the remainder breed in the far north, and a small population of Sandhill Cranes nests in the Intermountain West. Members of this family are threatened by wetland and grassland habitat destruction and degradation.

HERONS (family Ardeidae)

Wading birds of wetlands and grasslands, herons and egrets are patient, statue-like hunters that typically, and counterintuitively, nest in trees. Seen hunting in habitats as diverse as ocean surf, farm fields, and fresh- and saltwater wetlands, they employ hunting strategies to match the habitat and prey. Fish, amphibians, voles, mice, and snakes are all on the menu.

PLOVERS (family Charadriidae)

Many people think they must go to the coast to see plovers; however, they live at all elevations in open habitats from Arctic to alpine tundra and beach to desert. Only Antarctica lacks plovers. Invertebrates are captured using one hunting strategy, which, from the sidelines, appears as a game of red light, green light: run, stop, run, stop, probe, run. Long incubation periods produce chicks that, once hatched, are highly mobile and capable of feeding independently. Habitat loss and nest disturbance are the primary threats to plovers in the Pacific Northwest.

SANDPIPERS & ALLIES (family Scolopacidae)

Sometimes frustratingly similar in plumage and behavior, this large cosmopolitan family, the smallest members of which are called "peeps," displays a wide variety of bill and leg lengths to probe mud or sand for invertebrates. Breeding strategies are as varied as bill types, but most species nest in open wetlands and grasslands and winter in estuaries and bays. Nests are commonly on the ground, and chicks hatch ready to run. Uniquely, phalaropes forage in water and winter at sea in the tropics.

GULLS & TERNS (family Laridae)

The larids, as this family is commonly called, are a diverse family that spans the globe. Pacific Northwest larids are represented by gulls and terns, but the family also includes skimmers. Despite the old moniker "seagull," gulls are familiar almost everywhere, on the coast and off. Bold and opportunistic, they hunt, scavenge, or steal your lunch seemingly without remorse. More slender and agile terns, on the other hand, mostly plunge-dive for fish and keep to themselves unless intruders enter the breeding colony. All species are monogamous and colonial or semicolonial. Although chicks are well-developed at hatching, parents feed them until they leave the nest. Habitat destruction, including the loss of the Arctic polar ice cap, is the primary threat to these species.

VULTURES (family Cathartidae)

The New World vultures, which include condors, are a small family of scavengers that range from southern Canada to the tip of South America. Not known for their flight skills, these birds are, regardless, among the most adept soaring birds in the world. In keeping with their low-effort soaring, breeding habits are equally low-impact; vultures never build nests. Parenting elicits a more focused effort from both parents, and chicks are fed long past fledging.

OSPREY (family Pandionidae)

The cosmopolitan Osprey family is found on every continent except Antarctica. Even more intriguing, the Osprey is the family's only member. Once decimated by DDT, these fish specialists occupy any body of water large enough to hold prey. Their nests have caused electrical outages when built on power poles, so artificial nesting platforms are now a common sight in suitable habitats.

HAWKS & EAGLES (family Accipitridae)

Absent only from Antarctica, hawks and eagles fill most terrestrial habitats around the globe. The theme throughout this family is a hooked bill and strong talons. Diets and foraging habits are diverse, but most raptors are predators—some specialize in a single prey item, while others are generalists. Nests are often used in consecutive years and can reach epic proportions. Adult pairs work together to raise chicks, some of which are attended by the parents for a year after fledging. Persecution and pesticides have been the greatest threat to these species.

FALCONS (family Falconidae)

Although falcons are often grouped with raptors, as they are in this book, they are more closely related to parrots and songbirds. A widely distributed but relatively small family, most species live in open habitats where they forage for insect, mammal, and bird prey. Falcons are known for precision hunting on long, pointed wings that allow rapid, powerful flight.

DOVES & PIGEONS (family Columbidae)

This large family holds 348 species that span all but Antarctica and the more extreme northern regions of the globe. Primarily fruit and seed eaters, their unique ability to feed chicks with a substance secreted from the parent's digestive tract allows for an extended breeding season. Like the now-extinct Passenger Pigeon, some members of this family are colonial nesters; all build what loosely translates to a nest of sticks.

OWLS (family Strigidae)

Obligate carnivores, the 229 species of the owl family span the globe, apart from Antarctica. Most owls are nocturnal and have numerous special adaptations to facilitate hunting in the dark—specialized eyes, ears, feathers, and a 270-degree rotation of the head. Pairs do not build nests but use other species' abandoned nests and cavities as well as cliffs and buildings. Males feed the females during incubation, and eggs hatch asynchronously. Both adults care for the young as they begin to branch, moving away from the nest as they gain size and strength.

GOATSUCKERS (family Caprimulgidae)

Often overlooked because of their nocturnal lifestyle and highly effective camouflage, the almost 100 species of goatsuckers, also called nightjars, nonetheless range across all continents except Antarctica. Sometimes congregating in large late-summer flocks, nightjars are strictly aerial insectivores that hunt by sight despite being nocturnal. One or two eggs are laid directly on the ground or gravel roofs in populated areas and attended by both parents. Chicks can fly as early as 10 days after hatching.

KINGFISHERS (family Alcedinidae)

Best known as brilliant, streaking flashes of color that dive headfirst into water, the large kingfisher family also holds species that probe for invertebrates on the forest floor. Large, daggerlike bills and loud, raucous calls often distinguish members of this family. Many kingfishers excavate nest burrows in riverbanks and, in the Northern Hemisphere, defend breeding territories until ice-up.

WOODPECKERS (family Picidae)

Often berated for hammering on metal stovepipes and pounding holes in eaves and soffits, woodpeckers deserve exemption from our wrath for the marvelous adaptations they embody. Reinforced skulls and insect-seeking tongues that recoil around the brain and into an eye socket provide an exceptional ability to forage in any tree trunk. Additionally, woodpeckers rarely reuse excavated nest cavities, creating opportunities for other species to shelter and raise young.

JAYS, CROWS, & RAVENS
(family Corvidae)

The corvids, as this family is called, are loved and hated. Opportunistic, omnivorous, highly adaptable, and unnervingly intelligent, corvids often outwit the best of us in pursuit of garden bounty or unguarded snacks. Black or blue, crested or long tailed, the family likely evolved in Australia and Asia and radiated into most every available niche around the globe.

HUMMINGBIRDS (family Trochilidae)

Warp speed and incomparable agility, feisty defense of food sources, and extreme territoriality defy the hummingbird's status as the smallest bird on earth. A strictly New World family, hummingbirds survive on nectar with an occasional insect meal, and enter torpor to reduce metabolism sufficiently to survive the night or a cold spell. While females do all the work of building nests and raising young, males dazzle us with shimmering colors and aggressive behavior.

LARKS (family Alaudidae)

Only one of the 93 lark family species lives in the New World, and it stays strictly in North America. Found in most open habitats, larks feed on invertebrates, seeds, and grain. Relatively inconspicuous most of the year, males are wildly visible during breeding season when they launch into the sky and sing. Nests are a simple grass cup in a tussock or under a cow flop. Chicks can leave the nest as soon as 15 days after egg laying but may stay under parental care for another month.

SWIFTS (family Apodidae)

Widely distributed around the globe, swifts are the minute, terrestrial equivalent of albatrosses. Spectacular aerial insectivores, many swift species forage widely and only land to breed. Swifts attach their nests of mud, grass, and twigs, among other materials, to vertical surfaces with saliva, and both parents share chick-raising responsibilities. Swifts and swallows are in long-term decline.

SWALLOWS (family Hirundinidae)

Even more widely distributed than swifts, swallows similarly range the skies in search of insects. Found in open landscapes, often near water, swallows nest in riverbank burrows and on protected structures to which a mud nest can be attached. Along with swifts, swallows appear to be hardest hit by the ongoing changes and declines in insect prey. Erratic climatic patterns and agricultural and residential insecticides, including neonicotinoids, may be causing this.

CHICKADEES (family Paridae)

Year-round residents in the Pacific Northwest, chickadees chatter and flit through the forest canopy, gleaning insects from foliage and bark in summer. They commonly gather in winter flocks with kinglets, creepers, and nuthatches. Winter flocks rely more heavily on seeds and will cache food. All species are cavity nesters but rarely excavate nests.

KINGLETS (family Regulidae)

Six kinglet species range the temperate and boreal latitudes. Found year-round in the Pacific Northwest, they often flock with chickadees, creepers, and nuthatches in winter. Tiny energy powerhouses, kinglets are agile on the wing and flit between trees, sometimes hovering, to glean insects from bark and leaves. Females are the exclusive incubator, but both adults care for chicks for two to three weeks before fledging. The male continues feeding fledglings another three weeks after they leave the nest.

VIREOS (family Vireonidae)

Best known for their relentless repetitive singing, vireos are forest birds found through much of North and South America. The family also includes two disparate genera in Southeast Asia and the South Pacific. They glean insects from trees, hawk insects from the air, and eat berries and fruit. All vireos have heavy bills and an eyering or stripe.

FLYCATCHERS (family Tyrannidae)

The largest bird family, flycatchers are strictly New World birds. Highly diverse in habitat preferences, species have radiated into every niche without significantly changing appearance. Often best distinguished by call, flycatchers of genus *Empidonax* have been the identification nemesis of many birders, new and seasoned. Flycatchers are light, quick fliers that hunt from a stationary perch, launching into the air after insect prey.

SHRIKES (family Laniidae)

Songbirds turned hunters, shrikes are impressive predators. Shrikes prefer habitat edges and open grasslands, deserts, and forests. With the strong feet and heavy bill of a raptor, their diets vary from insects to vertebrates. After severing the spinal cord, prey is often skewered on thorns or barbed wire to hold it in place for dining. Only the female incubates eggs, but both adults care for nestlings.

WRENS (family Troglodytidae)

Eighty-five of the 86 species in this family live in North and South America. The remaining species is the only family representative in Asia and Europe. Long, intricate, and frequent songs are the hallmark of these tiny birds. Although blending in well in varying shades of brown, discreet barring, and matching eyebrow color, most wrens are hyperactive. Frequently cocking their tails, they give themselves away with song and motion.

DIPPERS (family Cinclidae)

An iconic bird of fast-moving streams, there are five dipper species scattered across midlatitude mountain ranges. An aquatic songbird, dippers dive, swim, and walk underwater on rocks and the streambed for invertebrates, fish larvae, eggs, and even freshwater crabs. Unfazed by winter, they remain on open water, moving to lower elevations only when hunting is restricted by ice. Their nests are mossy, round, and tucked into rocks and tree roots above rushing water.

STARLINGS (family Sturnidae)

Naturally found in Europe, North Africa, and Asia, starlings were successfully introduced around the world. This family, which includes mynas, holds an array of vivid, iridescent species that sometimes have wattles and long tails. Opportunistic in feeding and nesting, many species, like the North American introduced representative, European Starling, are cavity nesters and can displace native birds. Not beloved in North America, where the population is burgeoning, the European population of this species is in decline.

THRUSHES (family Turdidae)

Thrushes are found on every continent except Antarctica. Best known for songs of gossamer notes left lingering in the forest, the family includes brilliant bluebirds, demure forest thrushes, and extroverted American Robins. Found in most habitats, they typically forage on the ground for invertebrates but also hawk insects from the air, and many eat fruit seasonally.

WAXWINGS (family Bombycillidae)

With only three species worldwide, one North American, one Asian, and one that bridges the two continents, waxwings are one of the smallest bird families. Inconspicuous through breeding season, they are a dynamic force the rest of the year. Brilliantly colored, often in huge flocks, noisy, boisterous, and known to strip a tree of its fruit in minutes, they move when the food is depleted. These birds eat almost exclusively fruit—even chicks and juveniles rarely eat insects—and nest later than most other bird species to take advantage of the late-season abundance.

THRASHERS (family Mimidae)

The strictly New World mimics are vocal and present during breeding but soon evaporate into the underbrush and shadows once the season ends. Only mockingbirds, commonly maligned for singing through the night, stay visible. Long tailed, often long or curve billed, their songs range the gamut of songs and notes stolen from their surroundings. From shrubby habitat to open woodlands, scrub, and desert, these mimics are opportunistic omnivores. Most species are territorial, and adults share chick-rearing.

NUTHATCHES (family Sittidae)

Although this family holds only one genus, there are 28 species that span temperate latitudes and dip into Micronesia. Nuthatches are supremely adapted to foraging on tree trunks and are often seen moving headfirst down the bark or hanging upside down, gleaning insects from a branch. In northern winters, they switch to seeds and flock with chickadees, creepers, and kinglets. Cavity nesters, nuthatches sometimes, uniquely, build a mud or resin dam around the cavity entrance. Like other forest species, habitat loss is an ongoing threat to these birds.

CREEPERS (family Certhiidae)

Although a relatively small family holding only 11 species, inconspicuous creepers are distributed globally throughout temperate regions and parts of central and southern Africa. Always spiraling up tree trunks in pursuit of prey, they feed on invertebrates gleaned from bark. The male feeds the female during incubation, and both adults build the nest and care for chicks. As with other forest birds, loss of habitat is a pressing concern.

FINCHES (family Fringillidae)

The famous finches of Charles Darwin's evolutionary epiphany were as well suited to radiating across the globe as they were to filling niches in the Galapagos. Only Australia and Antarctica lack these varied, effervescent birds. Primarily fruit and seed eaters, species of this large, diverse family exhibit a wide array of bill adaptations. This diversity of bill shapes translates to specialization in food sources. Many species are highly nomadic, following seed crops, and many time their breeding to leverage the choice seed crop into successful fledglings.

SPARROWS & ALLIES (family Passerellidae)

This New World family holds many confusingly similar striped, brown species in the north, but also includes larger, more colorful birds in Central and South America. Extremely flexible in habitat use and food sources, sparrows are year-round residents throughout the United States. Readily seen from tundra to desert and everywhere in between, they are frequent feeder friends. While the female does most of the pre-hatching work, both parents tend chicks and continue care up to a month after chicks fledge.

CHAT (family Icteriidae)

Once thought to be an oddity in the warbler family, the chat has been promoted: it is now the sole species in its one-genus family. The Yellow-breasted Chat breeds across much of the US and Mexico and winters in Central America. Until recently, its reclusive habits kept it out of the limelight and far from the scrutiny of ornithological taxonomists.

BLACKBIRDS & ALLIES (family Icteridae)

Another New World family found across a surprising array of habitats, the blackbirds include their namesake blackbirds, as well as orioles, meadowlarks, and cowbirds. Primarily insectivores, some also feed on seeds and fruits. Some species are colonial breeders, and some cooperative. Nests are commonly an open cup, though some ground-nesting species build a roof. Other species, like the orioles, weave hanging nests that entirely enclose eggs and chicks. Still others, like cowbirds, are nest parasites, never building their own nest or tending chicks but leaving the work to unwitting host parents. Regardless of such notably variable life strategies sustaining survival, many are faced with the threat of habitat loss.

WARBLERS (family Parulidae)

The spring darlings of birders, New World warblers become an identification nemesis during fall migration when they lose their signature bright colors. Found in most habitats—forest, field, desert, or swamp—they can be inconspicuous despite their bright breeding plumage and are sometimes more easily identified by song. Most species forage for invertebrates in trees or on the ground. Building strikes, cat predation, and habitat loss are serious and cumulative threats to this family.

GROSBEAKS, TANAGERS & ALLIES (family Cardinalidae)

Found in the West only during breeding season, the cardinal family is found year-round through the rest of North America and south to central Argentina. Most species display vibrant reds, blues, or yellows, making no obvious effort to conceal themselves in their varied habitats. This family is strongly divided by preferred foods. Heavy, conical bills are associated with the seed- and fruit-eating side of the family, while more slender-billed members primarily forage for insects and fruit. Nests may be built anywhere in the vegetation strata, the female is the primary incubator, and typically both adults care for young until beyond fledging.

FIELD
GUIDE

Light adult (right).
Clean white head, body,
and wings. Black wingtips
distinct. Pink legs and bill.
Light juveniles (left). Dusky
gray head, body, and back.
Dark bill, feet, and legs.

**Dark morph or
Blue Snow Goose adult.**
Dark breast and back, wing
feathers scalloped with
white. Dark wingtips and
white underwing coverts.

Ross's Goose adult.
Notably smaller than
Snow; round head, pinkish
bill with gray base.

SNOW GOOSE

Anser caerulescens

Spectacular flocks of this winter resident create a blizzard of birds in agricultural fields and wildlife refuges. One of the most abundant waterfowl species in the world, the growing population benefits from increased agricultural activity along migratory routes and in winter habitat.

Migrants and winter residents feed in large flocks on open agricultural fields and marshes. Hundreds, sometimes thousands, of Snow Geese take flight noisily and simultaneously when disturbed.

Common migrant; regular in winter. Small numbers across eastern Washington and Oregon; large flocks at Umatilla, Malheur, and Klamath NWRs. Look for them at Columbia NWR, Potholes Reservoir, Wade Park, McNary Dam, McKay Creek NWR, Farewell Bend SP, Ladd Marsh WMA, and Wood River Wetland.

Distinct, individual *heank*. Flocks call loudly and insistently, creating a hard-to-miss cacophony.

Ross's Goose, smaller overall, head more rounded; most common near Klamath.

Adult.
Pink bill, feathers at base
and side of bill buffy yellow.

Adults.
In flight and on the ground,
legs distinctly orange, belly
speckled. Orange legs just
visible here at waterline.

GREATER WHITE-FRONTED GOOSE

Anser albifrons

Nearly circumpolar in distribution, this stylish Old World goose has a white forehead, pale wing coverts, dark belly and breast bars, black rump, and white undertail. Although populations are generally stable, it is threatened by oil development on breeding grounds and the degradation and loss of migratory and wintering habitats.

Pasture, marshy habitat. Grazes on seeds and grains, and aquatic and terrestrial plants. Often congregates in large flocks, sometimes with other goose species. Commonly migrates at night.

Common spring migrant; regular in fall. Look for them at Columbia, Toppenish, and McNary NWRs; Ladd Marsh WMA; Crooked River Wetlands Complex; Malheur and Klamath NWRs.

Multisyllable cackling laughter intermixed with storybook goose honks. Wing noise evident when flushed; air movement through feathers audible when flocks sideslip to landing.

Superficially like juvenile Snow Goose (page 63); dark bill color in Snow, pinkish in Greater White-fronted, distinguishes species.

LENGTH: 28" / WINGSPAN: 53"

Adults.
Large gray-brown goose with black neck and head, white chin strap, under-wing darker than body.

Adults.
Distinct white chin strap; long, all-black neck. Pale, buffy breast.

Cackling Goose.
Medium-sized gray-brown goose with black neck and head, distinct white chin strap and neck ring.

CANADA GOOSE

Branta canadensis

Once the quintessential sound of fall, Canada Geese have adapted well to expanding human habitats. Found on almost any waterbody, Canadas are visible and vocal for much of the year. Resident Northwest populations are joined by several Arctic migrant subspecies for the winter.

Lakes, ponds, and open water. Forages on expansive lawns, golf courses, and agricultural fields. Large, vociferous flocks and family groups.

Abundant year-round resident and migrant. Look for them at Granite and Alkali Lakes, Windust Park, Wawawai CP, Anatone Flats, Cold Springs NWR, Wallowa Lake, Willow Creek Reservoir, Priest Hole, Houston Lakes, Poison Creek Reservoir, Adel Ponds, Spring Lake, and Wood River Wetland.

The classic goose *honk*!

Smaller Cackling Geese (marginally larger than Mallards) similar, with indistinct neckband and namesake cackling call.

Adults.
White swan with long, delicate neck and peaked back. Yellow spot at base of long black bill. Bill somewhat concave.

Trumpeter Swan adults.
Notably larger than Tundra Swan. Rounded back. Black bill straight compared to Tundra. Color wash on head variable based on iron in water and mud of foraging habitat.

TUNDRA SWAN

Cygnus columbianus

An Arctic breeder, Tundra Swans are the most common North American swan species. Common migrants through eastern Washington and Oregon, family groups travel together, and chicks stay with their parents until returning to the Arctic breeding grounds.

In winter, commonly found on freshwater ponds and marshes. Feeds on emergent vegetation and waste grains in agricultural fields. Commonly mixes with Trumpeter Swans.

Common migrant November–March. Look for them at Montlake Park, Turnbull and McNary NWRs, Crooked River Wetlands Complex, Malheur NWR, Summer Lake and Klamath WAs.

Individual *kloo* calls, sometimes strung together. Large flocks cacophonous.

Larger Trumpeter Swans, an Oregon sensitive species, distinguished by longer bill with black base. Back less peaked. Calls distinctive.

Male.
Green crest slicked back like 1950s' hair, red eye. Pink, black, and white bill. White cheek and chin strap against black face. Buff flank and dark russet breast.

Female.
White eyering extends beyond eye to puffy semi-crest. Pale throat, brown-and-white speckled breast and flanks, dark brown back.

WOOD DUCK

Aix sponsa

The exquisite patterning, flashy colors, and droopy crest distinguish Wood Ducks from other ducks. A cavity nester, chicks leap, sometimes great distances, from the nest cavity to the mother calling from below.

Wooded swamps, ponds, sloughs, floodplain forest; occasionally in sageland stock ponds during migration. Agile in flight through trees and dense forest, perches in trees. On the water, often slips into vegetation, disappearing when approached. Uses existing cavities for nesting, readily accepts boxes; regularly produces two broods.

Year-round, though uncommon, resident. Look for them at Hideaway Lake, Sunnyside Park (Pullman), Poppoff Trail, Whitman Mission National Historic Site, Horn Rapids Dam, Toppenish NWR, Hot Lake, Clyde Holliday State RA, Drake Park, Putnam's Point, Page Springs Campground.

Male high-pitched *zweeee*; female gives repetitive *wok wok wok*.

Superficially like Harlequin Duck, rare on the East Side.

Males.
Cinnamon-colored head, breast, and wings. Black-and-buff patterning on back and scattered across breast and wings. Pale blue wing coverts evident in flight. Red eye, black bill.

Female and male.
Female much like other dabblers; larger bill, less distinct patterning than female Blue-winged. Plumage color of adult male unique among ducks.

Blue-winged male and female.
Male with gray head, white crescent between bill and eye distinct from Cinnamon male and female. Female Blue-winged more patterned overall than Cinnamon female, white at base of bill connects with pale throat.

CINNAMON TEAL

Spatula cyanoptera

One of the least abundant dabbling ducks in North America, and in steep decline, most Cinnamon Teals breed in the Great Basin and winter in Mexico. Unlike most ducks, males stay close to the nests until near hatching time.

Vegetated freshwater of all forms, including alkaline ponds. An omnivorous dabbler; tips up to feed. Explodes from the water surface into flight. Agile and rapid flight, often maneuvering tightly in small flocks. Nests well concealed in vegetation and approached by tunnel.

Common breeder, mid-March to September. Look for them at Potholes SP, Cow Lake, Panorama Ponds, Ladd Marsh WMA, Crooked River Wetlands Complex, Adel Ponds, and Goose and Borax Lakes.

Mostly quiet, squeaky *quek quek* and a snorty rattle.

Blue-winged Teal female less auburn brown than Cinnamon, white at base of bill and throat. When not in breeding plumage, male Cinnamon distinguished from Blue-winged by red eye color.

Male.
Long, broad, black shovel bill. White breast, rust flanks and belly. Iridescent green head, bright yellow eye.

Female.
Long, broad bill unique. Head, neck, breast, flanks, wings, and back variations on a theme: brown with patterning, some finely detailed, some bolder, some less distinct.

NORTHERN SHOVELER

Spatula clypeata

The distinct coloration, bill shape, and unique filter-feeding habit of this species make for a remarkable assemblage. A puddle duck, shovelers leap explosively into flight from the water in a single motion.

Open, shallow water with dense vegetation; common in managed water (wastewater, agriculture, rice fields). Shovelers filter-feed, swirling in circles to stir up insects, larvae, and crustaceans. In shallow water, may filter bottom sediments. Males are territorial during nesting but form postbreeding flocks.

Common year-round. Look for them at McCain's and Panorama Ponds, Bennington Lake, Quesna CP, Thief Valley and Chickahominy Reservoirs, Lake Ewauna, and Adel Ponds.

Chuckchuck chuckchuck; unique call, often heard.

Green-winged Teal (page 83) and Cinnamon Teal (page 73) males have same blue wing patch, making the three superficially similar; females of all species similar. Shoveler's unique bill and larger size definitive.

Male.
Breeding plumage includes chestnut breast and flanks, brilliant green eyestripe, and broad buffy forehead, soliciting the name "bald pate." Pale gray bill with black tip.

Female.
Delicate black stippling on tan head. Chestnut sides and scalloping on wing feathers. Pale gray bill with black tip.

Eurasian Wigeon male and female.
Male with rufous head and narrow pale forehead, body more gray than American male, pale chestnut breast. Female head and breast more speckled, back grayer and less patterned.

AMERICAN WIGEON

Mareca americana

Once a prairie pothole breeder, the American Wigeon population dropped significantly in the mid-1900s. Since the late 1980s, the population has rebounded and leveled at approximately two-thirds of what it once was.

Marshes, ponds, agricultural land, shortgrass prairie. Forms large flocks; commonly mixes with Mallards, pintails, and Green-winged Teal. Quick to steal another duck's meal; feeds on insects and surface water plants. Often grazes on land.

Common migrant and winter resident late August–April. Look for them at Turnbull NWR, Lenore and Texas Lakes, Scooteney Reservoir, Alpowa Creek, Port Kelley, Sundale Park, Haystack and Poison Creek Reservoirs, Summer Lake WA, and Klamath NWR.

Females produce hoarse quack quack; male call surprisingly high, whistled *wheeWHEEwhe*.

Eurasian Wigeon sometimes found among American flocks. Male's rufous head, female's lack of white wing coverts, and gray underwing on both sexes distinguish Eurasian Wigeon from American.

LENGTH: 20" / WINGSPAN: 32"

Male and female.
Male with iridescent green head. White neck ring, russet breast. Pale gray flanks finely barred. Bill always yellow. Dark rump with curled tail feathers. Female with fine all-over patterning. Eyestripe; pale head and pale undertail. Bill often edged with orange or olive with dark center. Female's violet-blue wing patch not always evident; juveniles similar.

Gadwall male and female.
Female similar to Mallard hen, paler, lacks black eyestripe and black band on bill; bill smaller, orange along outside edge. Gray male Gadwall not like Mallard. Breeding male's head shape unique, appears puffy and angular.

MALLARD

Anas platyrhynchos

The most recognizable duck species, and the source of domestic ducks, Mallards have a cosmopolitan distribution made greater by introductions and vagrancy. It is the ubiquitous and quintessential dabbling duck.

Almost any body of water will host Mallards, city parks to farmyards, remote swamps to estuaries. Feeds on plants and invertebrates in water and on land; commonly seen bottoms up. Often flocks with other ducks.

Common year-round resident and migrant. Look for them at Reardan Ponds, Morgan Lake, Lyons Ferry and Cottonwood Canyon SPs, Little Willow Creek Reservoir, Clyde Holliday State RA, Adel Ponds, and Hagelstein Park.

Female Mallards give the classic duck quack. Male quacks higher pitched and burry. Call is a rapid and varied clucking.

Female Mallard like other dabbling duck females. Blue-and-white speculum and black-speckled orange bill unique. Female Gadwall less heavily patterned with white speculum.

LENGTH: 23" / WINGSPAN: 35"

Male.
Dark head distinct. Blue-gray and black bill. Slender neck with bright white throat and white stripe wrapping from throat up neck to back of head. White breast, fine gray patterning on flanks, buffy sides of rump, long central tail feathers. Males up to 25" in length.

Females.
Buffy tan back and wings, pale belly with sparse patterning. No markings on head; gray bill. Noticeably smaller than male.

Males.
Elongated shape distinct in flight.

NORTHERN PINTAIL

Anas acuta

The stately Northern Pintail is more upright and graceful than most waterfowl. An early prairie and tundra nester, pintails are one of the first migrants to return in fall. Half of the North American pintail population was lost to habitat changes and agricultural practices over the last 50 years.

Shallow wetlands and flooded agricultural land. Feeds on waste grains, tubers, seeds, and invertebrates. Often in large flocks and mixed with other dabblers.

Common migrant, occasional breeder, regular in winter. Look for them at Philleo and Lenore Lakes, Columbia NWR, Alpowa Creek, Cold Springs NWR, Haystack Reservoir, Silvies Valley, North Beede Reservoir, Malheur NWR, Hart Lake, Lake Abert, and Klamath NWR.

Male display call is a whistled, ascending *zzzzzOOP*; female gives hoarse, high-pitched *quack*.

Female like other dabblers; slender neck, unmarked head, and dark bill distinct.

Male.
Rufous head with dark green from eye to nape. Distinctive white vertical band seems misplaced on side of breast. Buffy hip patch.

Female.
The smallest teal and like other dabblers. Dark eyeline, pale buff streak on tail.

Blue-winged Teal male.
White crescent at bill base separates it from Green-winged Teal and is the easiest characteristic for distinguishing them in flight.

GREEN-WINGED TEAL

Anas crecca

The smallest dabbler, Green-winged Teal is a cosmopolitan species that breeds in forested wetlands and river deltas. Although still one of the most common ducks, the current population is less than half that of the mid-1900s.

Freshwater ponds, marshes, and agricultural lands. Often feeds hidden in emergent vegetation; more evident when foraging on open mudflats. Explosive flier leaps directly into the air and performs evasive maneuvers.

Common migrant and winter resident; uncommon breeder. Look for them at Philleo Lake, Gloyd Seeps Wetland, Scooteney Reservoir, Bennington Lake, Manns Pond, Deschutes River State RA, Ochoco Lake CP, North Beede Reservoir, Borax Lake, and Lakes Abert and Ewauna.

Males give sharp, discrete *chIRP*, sometimes in a series. Female produces husky *quack*.

Rare winter visitor Eurasian (Common) Teal mixes with Green-winged flocks. Female Blue-winged and Cinnamon Teal (see page 73) similar.

LENGTH: 14" / WINGSPAN: 23"

Male and female.
Male with rust-red head, black breast, pale gray and rounded back, dark tertials. Female pale brown with little patterning, eyering, buffy cheek. Both pale blue-gray bill with black tip.

Canvasback male.
Long, black, angled bill. Dark forehead, red eye, rust throat and nape. Brown-black breast; bright gray-white back.

Canvasback female.
Buff head, neck, and breast. Back lighter. Long, black, angled bill. Faint white eyeline from back edge of eye.

REDHEAD

Aythya americana

Male Redheads are contortionists, extending their heads backward to lie between their wings in breeding displays. Female Redheads are sometimes nest parasites when water conditions are unfavorable.

Shallow and ephemeral wetlands, lakes, marshes. Often seen with other ducks. Feeds on aquatic vegetation and invertebrates. Nests in dense, vegetated wetland margins. Leaps out of the water to arc into a dive. Runs to take off from water and skids to halt when landing.

One of the East Side's most common breeding ducks; relatively common migrant. Look for them at Cheney Wetlands, Steamboat Rock SP, Columbia NWR, Hatfield Lake, Dry Lake Reservoir, and Summer Lake and Klamath WAs.

WHIRrrrr, soft quacks.

Canvasback male darker head, whiter back and flanks. Canvasback's sloped forehead at same angle as bill; Redhead's bill and forehead distinct. Female Redhead more uniform brown than Canvasback.

Male.
Unique head shape and black back, white vertical band between black breast and gray flank. White outline at base of bill, white ring around bill, black tip. Ring around the neck barely visible under the best circumstances.

Female.
White eyering faintly extends to back of head. Feathers at base of bill pale. Body evenly brown. Faint wingbar in flight.

Greater Scaup male.
Larger than Ring-neck and Lesser Scaup. Back pale gray with delicate barring, white flanks. Black breast and rear. Bill uniform gray with black nail.

Greater Scaup female.
Round head and distinct white at base and sides of bill. Darker head than Ring-neck female. Bill black.

RING-NECKED DUCK

Aythya collaris

Better named "Ring-*billed* Duck," the generalized diet of Ring-necked Ducks likely contributed to their late-twentieth century range expansion. Unlike most divers, Ring-necks leap directly into flight, allowing use of small, wooded waterbodies.

Shallow freshwater marshes. Nests on wooded ponds. Forages underwater for plants and insects. Launches upward from water with wings tight against the body before folding over and plunging underwater.

Fairly common breeder; common migrant and winter resident, especially along Columbia River. Look for them at Gardner Road Wetlands, Jameson Lake, Quincy WA, Port of Arlington, Ladd Marsh WMA, Poison Creek Reservoir, Summer Lake and Klamath WAs.

Males sound much like a squeaky toy; female call resembles a raven-duck hybrid *quack*.

Lesser and Greater Scaup females with more distinct white patch at bill base. Scaup males with pale back and minimal crest. All scaup lack ring on bill.

Male.
Bold white wedge at back of head unmistakable. In good light, green forehead, iridescent eggplant-colored neck. Black back. White breast and flanks, wing patches, and back of head.

Female.
Dark brown head, white cheek patches with indistinct edges extending toward back of head. Dark back, buffy tan breast.

BUFFLEHEAD

Bucephala albeola

The smallest diving duck, Buffleheads preferentially nest in old Northern Flicker cavities in boreal forest and aspen stands. Forest clearing for agriculture and logging changed breeding distribution; however, Buffleheads will use nest boxes, and their population appears stable.

Regularly in small flocks, uses smaller waterbodies than most ducks. Avoids vegetated ponds and large lakes. Runs on water for takeoff. Winters primarily on saltwater. Feeds on insects, crustaceans, and mollusks in shallow water, rarely over submerged vegetation.

Common migrant and winter resident. Look for them at Lenore and Crooked Knee Lakes, Hatton Coulee Rest Area, Steptoe Canyon, Wade, Crow Butte, and Celilo Parks, Poison Creek Reservoir, Malheur NWR, Borax Lake, and Lower Klamath Lake Road.

Individual repeated croaking *quacks*.

The larger Common and Barrow's Goldeneyes (page 91) have white patches in front of eye; females lack white patch.

Male.
Dark green head, sometimes appears black, round white spot at bill base. White flanks, white secondaries edged with thin black dividers. High, back-sloping forehead.

Female.
Gray-brown back, chocolate-colored head with brilliant golden eye and mostly dark bill.

Barrow's Goldeneye male.
Crescent-shaped white patch in front of eye compared with Common male's round white spot below eye. More extensive black back than Common with distinct white spots along secondaries.

Barrow's Goldeneye female.
Darker, rounder head, steeper forehead; smaller bill more yellow than Common's.

COMMON GOLDENEYE

Bucephala clangula

Boreal-forest cavity nesters, Common Goldeneyes have a complex social structure and may not breed until their third or fourth year. Environmental degradation impacts are rapidly evident, potentially making these diving ducks a good bioindicator species.

Known for brood parasitism—females regularly lay eggs in other ducks' nests. Spectacular male breeding display begins in fall. Winters on open freshwater with sandy and gravelly bottoms, foraging for fish, crustaceans, and mollusks.

Common migrants and winter residents. Look for them at Putters and West Medical Lakes, Washtucna, Boyer and Rooks Parks, Port of Arlington, Wallowa Lake and Cove Palisades SPs, Summer Lake WA, Lake Ewauna, and Antelope Reservoir.

Male, *peent peent* accompanied by insect-like rasp; female makes piglike grunts.

Steep forehead, smaller bill, crescent-shaped white patch distinguish Barrow's Goldeneye, which is often found among Commons.

LENGTH: 18.5" / WINGSPAN: 26"

Male.
Long, narrow bill, rust flanks. Open crest reveals wedge-shaped white patch. Fully closed crest appears as white stripe extending behind eye.

Female.
Gray overall. Crest spiky, punk, red-brown when open; elongates head when closed.

HOODED MERGANSER

Lophodytes cucullatus

Hooded Mergansers are North America's smallest and only endemic merganser. A woodland species, Hoodies are indiscriminate in their choice of forest type and readily use nest boxes on poles. They do, however, prefer waterfront property and water below the nest.

Nests and winters on wooded freshwater ponds and streams. Opportunistic feeders that take fish, insects, and crustaceans, especially crayfish. Cavity nester. Like goldeneyes, they are brood parasites.

Uncommon but widespread breeder; common fall migrant and wintering duck; will stay until freeze-up. Look for them at Sheep, Alkali, and Hideaway Lakes, Potholes SP, Two Rivers Park, Thief Valley Reservoir, Summer Lake WA, and Lower Klamath NWR.

Repeated crow-like call; display call similar to deep-throated toad, rolled and raspy *RrrRrrrrrrRrrr*.

Male Hooded Merganser's narrow bill, yellow eye, rust flanks distinguish it from male Bufflehead (page 89).

Male.
Elongated green head; green throat. Red bill. White breast, collar, and flanks. Dark back.

Female.
Elongated, dark rust-colored head, bright white breast and throat. Bill pale salmon color.

Red-breasted Merganser male.
Ragged green crest, white neckband, rusty-brown breast unique among mergansers. Long, fine orange-red bill, not as heavy as Common's.

Red-breasted Merganser female.
Tan and gray neck and breast distinct from white breast of Common female. Long, fine orange-red bill.

COMMON MERGANSER

Mergus merganser

Less common than Red-breasted Mergansers, Commons breed in the northern hemisphere midlatitudes, wintering across the US. Primarily feeding on fish, they serve as bio-indicators for pesticides and heavy metals that accumulate up the food chain.

Forested lake, river habitat. Often hunts with head submerged. Flies low and fast over open water. Cavity nester. Short-distance migrants, they often arrive early and leave late, sometimes wintering on open water in the far north.

Common year-round resident. Look for them at Sprague Lake, Dry Falls, Burkett Lake RA, McNary NWR, Rhinehart Canyon, Crooked River Wetlands Complex, Summer Lake WA, Catlow Valley Road.

Female makes quiet, repeated *caw*; displaying males produce seemingly digitally altered frog call, splashes.

Red-breasted Merganser appears disheveled compared to Common, red eye, notable crest; red head of female Red-breasted ends in less distinct line at gray neck.

LENGTH: 25" / WINGSPAN: 34"

Breeding male.
Bright cinnamon-red body, black head, white cheek, blue bill, jaunty tail. Unmistakable.

Breeding female.
Dark cap includes eye, parallel white and dark bands below eye. Dark bill and back. Tail often cocked, white undertail coverts.

Nonbreeding pair.
Both with white cheeks, overall dark brown. Male's blue bill less vibrant but evident.

RUDDY DUCK

Oxyura jamaicensis

Male Ruddy Ducks are unmistakable with a blue bill and stiff, pointy, often upright tail. Females build nests over water, weave a roof from surrounding vegetation, and raise the nest floor if water levels rise. Like grebes, the legs are set far back on the body, making Ruddy Ducks awkward on land. A thoroughly unique and engaging bird.

Breeds on marshes, seasonal wetlands. Forages for invertebrates. Requires long, running takeoff from water. Flight fast and direct. Nests in dense cattails and bulrushes. Often aggressive toward other Ruddy Ducks and waterfowl.

Common breeder and migrant. Look for them at Cheney Wetlands, Swanson Lakes WA, Soap Lake, Ginkgo Petrified Forest SP, Buena Pond, Warehouse Beach RA, Bennington Lake, McKay Creek NWR, Bliss Road Wetland, Crooked River Wetlands Complex, and Adel Ponds.

Like a frog stifling a sneeze.

None regionally.

Adult.
Overall gray, head darker. Red eye. White bill with burnt red forehead shield and black band at tip. Short tail with white tail streaks. Thick yellow-green legs, huge feet.

AMERICAN COOT

Fulica americana

Technically not waterfowl, the American Coot is a member of the rail family. But unlike most rails, which are seldom seen, coots are often on open water and form rafts of hundreds in winter. Look overhead for eagles hunting the flock.

Freshwater wetlands with emergent vegetation; requires standing water for nesting. Heads bob in unison when walking and swimming. Omnivorous, mostly aquatic plants, also invertebrates, small fish, tadpoles. Requires long, running takeoff; awkward in flight; webbed and lobed feet well adapted to diving and walking on marshy vegetation. Will graze on grass and in agriculture.

Common year-round resident and migrant. Look for them at Fishtrap RA, Hideaway Lake, Central Ferry HMU, Sarg Hubbard and Davis Creek Parks, Christmas Valley, and Spring and Borax Lakes.

Variable squeaks, tin-horn honks, clucks, pips.

None. White bill on all-black bird distinctive.

Male.
Black throat outlined in white. Light, streaked forehead with white dividing line below plume and dark cap. Fine, pointed scaling on neck. Back gray, wings gray with white streaks. Belly heavily scaled, buff feathers with dark center line and edging. Belly center with burnt red scales, black trim.

Female.
Gray back, brown wings with white edging. Neck pattern sharp and fine-scaled. Breast gray, belly scaled with white feathers rimmed in brown. Topknot dainty compared to male's showy plume.

CALIFORNIA QUAIL

Callipepla californica

Native to California and Baja, California Quail have expanded their range north and east and have been widely introduced. Commonly seen scurrying through the brush in small groups, their bouncing topknots and endless chatter make them a delight.

Sagebrush, dry oak forest, brushy and riparian areas; ranches, parks, small towns. Mostly runs; a few birds will fly at a time when startled, leapfrogging. Covey remains consistently in vocal contact. Maintains year-round home range with seasonal movement. Omnivorous, fruit, seeds, flowers, leaves, insects.

Common year-round. Look for them at Reardan Ponds, Northrup Canyon, Ephrata Cemetery, Crab Creek Road WA, Whitcomb Island, Wallowa Fish Hatchery, Davis Creek Park, Crooked River Wetlands Complex, Hagelstein Park, and Page Springs Campground.

Single note *caw*; location call *she-Ka-doh*.

Mountain Quail rare; long crown feathers lay back or upright. Introduced Gray Partridge and Chukar uncommon; both lack topknot.

Male.
Naked head and neck blue with red bumps. Scraggly horsetail-like beard emerges directly from base of throat. Feathers iridescent green, bronze, shimmery red. Primaries checkered white and brown. Tail feathers rufous tipped.

Female.
Notably smaller than male. Naked head and neck. Feathers less brilliantly iridescent. Lacks beard.

Displaying males fan tails and hold body feathers erect. Skin around eye more vibrant blue. Bulbous, red, warty wattle hangs from lower jaw, and fleshy snood, a flap of skin, hangs from forehead over bill.

WILD TURKEY

Meleagris gallopavo

Native to North America, Wild Turkeys were widely eradicated and reintroduced. Now found throughout much of
the Pacific Northwest, these flocks were established from
Eastern stock.

Open, mature mixed forest; shrubby meadows and edges.
Flies to roost but forages on the ground. Scratches for
seeds and nuts in winter; grasses, invertebrates, small
vertebrates in summer. Males perform elaborate spring
displays for breeding rights but don't contribute to incubation or chick-rearing.

Common year-round except in southeast Oregon, where
largely absent. Look for them at Turnbull NWR, Banks
Lake, Alpowa Creek, Chief Joseph WRA, McNary NWR,
Rager Ranger Station, Succor Creek State Natural Area.

Male breeding song *GabbaGabbaGab*. Call terse, high
and rising *tirk, tirk, tirk*.

None. Male turkeys significantly bigger than females—
wingspan 14" longer, and weight up to 7 pounds more.
Female length and wingspan given.

Male.
Red facial skin surrounded by iridescent purple and green throat and neck, white neckband. Pale bill. Back tawny, shimmery wings green and brown, rump pale gray. Long brown tail with black bars unique.

Female.
Pale throat and under-eye eye-liner. Overall buffy tan with dark chevron patterning. Patterning continues on long tail.

RING-NECKED PHEASANT

Phasianus colchicus

A popular game bird, Ring-necked Pheasants were first intro-duced from Asia in the late 1800s. Commonly seen in wheat fields and along roadsides, the male with its flashy green head and long tail is distinctive.

Shrubby wetland and forest edges, roadsides and agri-cultural land with dense cover. Forages on the ground for grain and grasses, fruit, nuts, insects. Strong and explo-sive flier but tends to walk or run to cover.

Relatively common year-round resident; rare in south-east Oregon. Look for them at Reardan Ponds, Sprague Lake, Columbia and Umatilla NWRs, Crooked River Wetlands Complex, and Lower Klamath NWR.

Scratchy *WATwat* followed by wing whirr. Call is hiccup-like.

None. Long tail feathers on males and females unique. Males as much as 14" longer than female length.

Breeding adult.
Small, reddish brown bird with dark
eye, white eyering. Short, thick, whitish
gray bill with black band. Shows little
seasonal color variation; black bill
band absent in nonbreeding plumage.

PIED-BILLED GREBE

Podilymbus podiceps

"Threatened," "endangered," "in need of conservation," "imperiled" all apply to the Pied-billed Grebe in the East. Thankfully, in the Pacific Northwest, this small grebe has a stable population and is visible on many waterbodies year-round.

Builds floating nests in freshwater wetlands and ponds with emergent vegetation; winters on fresh and salt water. Rarely flies in daylight. Opportunistic feeder, dives for fish, insects, amphibians, and crayfish. Often lurks in emergent vegetation, evaporating out of sight either into plants or by submerging all but its head.

Common year-round resident. Look for them at Rock and Osborn Bay Lakes, Ginkgo Petrified Forest SP, Crow Butte Park, Wallowa Lake SP, Crooked River Park, Malheur NWR, Roaring Springs Ranch, and Shoalwater Bay.

Loud, gurgling *whowhowhwowho* and *who hoop who hoop*. Indescribable and unmistakable.

Distinguished from other grebes by compact size, short neck, stout bill.

Breeding adult. Black cap with solid buff-yellow eyestripe swept back to crest. Short, thick bill.

Nonbreeding adult. Bright white cheek, white throat and neck. Head dusky gray, back mottled gray. Red eye appears to bleed into pale gray bill.

Breeding Eared Grebe. Crest more defined, back of head less angular than Horned; lores (feathers between bill and eye) black.

Nonbreeding Eared Grebe. Mostly gray, pale neck, less defined cheeks, gray bill. Compare with white cheek and neck in Horned Grebe.

HORNED GREBE

Podiceps auritus

Horned Grebes breed across northern North America, Scandinavia, and Siberia. Despite its wide distribution, Horned Grebe numbers are in long-term decline, and the global population is designated as Vulnerable.

Winters on big rivers and open water. Dives for bottom fish and invertebrates. Remarkable feet and leg mobility allow use as oars underwater. Sometimes forms large flocks before migration. Takes on full breeding plumage before migrating to nesting grounds.

Common winter resident and migrant August–April. Mostly absent from southeast Oregon. Rare breeder. Look for them at Rock Lake, Turnbull NWR, Frenchman Coulee, Riverview Park, Port of Arlington, Wallowa Lake, Prineville Reservoir, and Moore Park.

Mostly silent in winter.

Nonbreeding Eared Grebe distinguished by smaller, upturned bill; crest centered forward on head versus Horned Grebe crest at back of head.

Breeding adult. Overall darker than nonbreeding birds. Eye surrounded by black, rather than gray in nonbreeding birds.

Nonbreeding adult. Long, slightly upcurved, yellow-olive bill. Thin black stripe down back of neck; throat and breast white. Eye entirely surrounded by gray.

Breeding Clark's Grebes. Eye surrounded by white. Bill more yellow-orange, less olive than Western.

WESTERN GREBE

Aechmophorus occidentalis

Best known for their elaborate mating displays, Western Grebe pairs run across the water in sync. With necks elongated, heads forward, and bills skyward, the intent is unmistakable.

Colonial nester on fresh water with open water and bordering vegetation; winters on salt water. Opportunistic, feeds almost exclusively on a wide variety of fish species. Like other grebes, dives to forage, swims underwater using both feet, rarely flies outside of migration, and migrates nocturnally. Sometimes forms large winter flocks.

Common but local summer resident; regularly winters on Columbia River. Look for them at Moses Lake, Potholes and Ginkgo Petrified Forest SPs, Big Flat HMU, Port of Arlington, Union Creek Campground, Ochoco Lake CP, Malheur NWR, Antelope Reservoir, Adel Ponds, Lake Ewauna Nature Trail.

High-pitched cricket-like chirps.

Cap on rare Clark's Grebe does not surround eye like Western's.

Breeding adult.
Crest may be all dark, all white, or salt-and-pepper, like this bird. Sky-blue gape, green eye, and yellow skin are irresistible. Iridescent green-black feathers; mottled black-and-white bill.

Immature.
Pale throat and breast, dark belly and back. Yellow-orange lores.

DOUBLE-CRESTED CORMORANT

Nannopterum auritum

Although pollutants caused the Double-crested Cormorant population to crash in the early 1970s, these diving birds have rebounded exponentially. Now found across North America, they often dive into trouble with fisheries.

Fresh waterbodies large enough for lengthy takeoff with feeding, loafing, and roosting areas. Forages for fish using webbed toes for propulsion. Often seen perched with wings spread. Flies in rough flocks.

Common year-round resident on Columbia River; fairly common winter resident and migrant. Look for them at Saltese Flats, Sprague Lake, Dry Falls, Priest Rapids Lake, Bateman Island, Morgan Lake, Houston Lakes, Chickahominy Reservoir, Summer Lake WA, and Upper Klamath Lake.

Breeding birds grunt, like children playing burping games.

The only cormorant commonly found on freshwater.

LENGTH: 33" / WINGSPAN: 52"

Adult.
American White Pelicans use their voluminous pouches to scoop up prey, tipping their heads back to swallow fish whole.

Adults.
Large size and a massive bill make pelicans unmistakable. White body and wings, black flight feathers.

AMERICAN WHITE PELICAN

Pelecanus erythrorhynchos

Commonly seen along the Columbia River, American White Pelicans are returning to their previous haunts and expanding their range. The greatest threat pelicans face is habitat loss.

Regularly forage collectively in lakes using movement to concentrate small fish species, scooping prey from the upper water column into pouches. Barely visible flocks glide long distances at high altitudes.

Fairly common year-round; less so in southeast Oregon, especially in winter. Wallula breeding colony reestablished in the early 1990s. Look for them at Hog and Cow Lakes, Washtucna, McNary and Umatilla NWRs, Ladd Marsh, Houston Lakes, Malheur NWR, Summer Lake WA, and Klamath NWR.

Adults make a frog-like grunt on the breeding grounds, but birds are otherwise mostly silent.

Brown Pelicans rival White Pelicans in size and shape but are rare away from the coast.

LENGTH: 62" / WINGSPAN: 108"

Adults

All gray plumage in winter; summer adults more rust-brown. Red crown. Tail bustle. Long, dark bill. Neck always elongated.

Immature.

Rust-brown back fades by end of first winter. Back of head and neck also rust-brown. Indistinct red around eyes.

SANDHILL CRANE

Antigone canadensis

Known for flocking in the thousands during migration, Sandhill Cranes are most often seen in pairs or small family groups. Cranes are typically long-lived, and Sandhills can live into their thirties.

Wetlands, grasslands. Omnivorous and opportunistic. Picks prey from vegetation; probes while walking through open grasslands and wet meadows. Flies with neck and legs outstretched.

Common spring and fall migrant. Regular breeder at Malheur NWR and Summer Lake WA. Look for them at Turnbull NWR, Sun Lakes SP, Quincy WA, Scooteney Reservoir, Toppenish and Cold Springs NWRs, Crooked River Wetlands Complex, North Beede Reservoir, Page Springs Campground, Hart and Borax Lakes, and Bliss Road Wetland.

Throaty, clacking, echoing; rolled Rs and chatter. Heard from great distances.

Great Blue Heron (page 119) has black head plumes, white forehead, orange bill; no brown in body plumage; flies with neck pulled in.

LENGTH: 46" / WINGSPAN: 77"

Adult.
Often motionless for extended periods, hunched and with long neck held tightly to body. Long legs allow wading in deep water.

Adult
Yellow, daggerlike bill. Black-and-white stripes on head extend into flowing plumes. Neck snakelike.

Great Egret adult.
Smaller, all white; yellow bill, black legs.

GREAT BLUE HERON

Ardea herodias

Whether hunting in a wetland or a farmer's field, the long-legged, long-necked Great Blue Heron is a familiar sight. Slow-moving when stalking, lightning fast when striking, Great Blue Herons are usually solitary hunters but nest colonially in rookeries.

Wetlands, fields, meadows. Forages for fish, crustaceans, amphibians, voles, and snakes. Nests in trees within range of primary foraging grounds.

Common year-round resident. Look for them at Gardner Road Wetlands, Coulee City and Rooks Parks, McKay Creek NWR, LaPage Park, Sherars Falls, Smith Rock SP, Riley Pond, Catlow Valley Road, Adel Ponds, and Moore Park.

Loud, croaking grunts often given in flight or when startled from water's edge.

Sandhill Cranes (page 117) more gray-brown, adults with noticeable red crown; rarely alone. Cranes fly with outstretched neck; Great Blue Herons curve neck into their shoulders. Uncommon Great Egrets notably smaller, entirely white.

Adult.
Two black bands unique among plovers. White belly, brown back, long tail. Rufous rump.

Breeding male Semipalmated Plover.
Dark brown head with black eye mask. White neckband and black collar complete. Dark brown back, yellow-orange legs and bill with black tip. Female similar, less bold coloring.

KILLDEER

Charadrius vociferus

One of the most visible and vocal shorebirds anywhere, this plover is well adapted to humans and is a common fixture on gravel roads and rooftops, as well as beaches and sandbars.

Varied open landscapes often far from water: pastures, parking lots, gravel roofs, and expansive lawns. Forages on the ground for invertebrates. Nests in loose gravel or sand in the open; distracts humans and predators from nests and chicks with a broken-wing act. Forms small flocks in winter.

Common year-round resident. Look for them at Stutler-Smythe Road Wetlands, Reardan Ponds, Steamboat Rock SP, Soap Lake, Burkett Lake RA, Toppenish NWR, Anatone Flats, Ladd Marsh WMA, Houston Lakes, North Beede and Antelope Reservoirs, Lake Abert, Klamath WA.

KiDeeKiDeeKiDeeKiDee ad infinitum and *Ki Ki Ki Ki Kiii Ki Ki Ki Kiii*.

Semipalmated Plover smaller, less rufous, single dark breastband.

Adult.
Long red legs distinct. Long, sharp
bill. White eyebrow. Black head, neck,
back, and tail. White forehead and
face, throat, breast, and belly.

BLACK-NECKED STILT

Himantopus mexicanus

Appearing somewhat hunchbacked in flight, Black-necked Stilts are graceful waders. Crisp black-and-white bodies, long red legs, disproportionately large eyes, and a precise black bill make stilts unmistakable.

Shallow wetlands, flooded lowlands, saline ponds. Forages for invertebrates in water column and mud by plucking and scything; also snatches insects from air. Often nests in slightly elevated wetland vegetation stubble. Vocal and flustered when territory is breached. Often seen with American Avocets (page 124).

Local summer resident through August; most evident in April and May. Look for them at Reardan Ponds, Soap Lake, Potholes SP, Bateman Island, Manns Pond, Crooked River Wetlands Complex, Hatfield Lake, Chickahominy and Antelope Reservoirs, Hart Lake, and Wood River Wetland.

One- and two-syllable *piPip* or *PipPipPip*.

No similar species in North America.

Male.
Long, upturned bill. Soft, rufous head, neck, and breast. Black wings with wide, horizontal white bar. Long, pale gray legs.

Female.
Overall pattern same as but paler than male. Bill more strongly curved.

AMERICAN AVOCET

Recurvirostra americana

American Avocets have an affinity for salt and alkaline ephemeral spring ponds. Shallow waterbodies with salt-crusted beaches and plants specially adapted to them provide food and nesting sites in what appear to be inhospitable locations.

Shallow wetlands, playas. Forages for invertebrates mainly by sweeping long, curved bill through water. Nests on the ground in the open, often along dikes and gravel roads.

Local, common April to September. Look for them at Turnbull NWR, Scooteney Reservoir, Sunnyside WRA, Duffy's Pond, Potholes SP, Umatilla NWR, Thief Valley Reservoir, Crystal Crane Hot Springs, Chickahominy and Rock Creek Reservoirs, Summer Lake WA, Bliss Road Wetland, and Klamath NWR.

High-pitched, repetitive *peep* or *plee*. Can be chatty and goose-like.

Distinctly different from and commonly seen with Black-necked Stilts (page 123); otherwise, no similar species.

Adult.
Very long downcurved bill. Gray legs. Uniform streaking on head. Back tan-and-brown chevron-like pattern. Throat, breast, and belly reddish buff.

Nonbreeding adult Long-billed Dowitcher.
Half the size of curlew. Bill heavier, shorter, and straight compared to curlew. Overall grayer; patterning on back heavier, less uniform than curlew. Back white in flight.

LONG-BILLED CURLEW

Numenius americanus

A grassland-breeding shorebird, the Long-billed Curlew is an oddity in dry, open landscapes across the Intermountain West. Often heard long before being sighted, males are extremely territorial and take full responsibility for chicks soon after hatching.

Open grassland, wheat stubble, grassy areas in sagebrush desert. Commonly seen roadside in open agriculture. Nests on the ground in clumpy vegetation. Strolls through open fields, often in pairs, male will flutter-fly and call incessantly when disturbed near nest.

Local, uncommon but regular; mid-March–early August. Winters mainly in Mexico. Look for them at LaCrosse, Gloyd Seeps Wetland, 9 Mile Canyon Road, Umatilla NWR, North Powder Pond, Paulina Valley, Lawen Marshes, Paulina Marsh, Malheur NWR, Paisley, and Klamath Marsh NWR.

High-pitched, piercing *Q-i Q-i*. Chattering alarm *qiqiqiqi*.

Long-billed Dowitcher half as large, bill shorter and straight.

LENGTH: 23" / WINGSPAN: 35"

Breeding adult.
Rufous cap, ear, and wing. Spotted throat and breast, extending to flanks. Long black bill, slightly downcurved.

Nonbreeding adult.
Overall paler than breeding bird. Bright white breast with faint collar.

Late-season breeding Least Sandpiper.
Short, slightly drooped bill. Brown-and-rufous scaled back.

Breeding Semipalmated Sandpiper.
Short, straight black bill. Overall more gray than Western and Least, and between the two in size.

WESTERN SANDPIPER

Calidris mauri

Sometimes found in flocks of thousands during migration on the coast, Western Sandpipers are seen in more modest numbers on the East Side. Males winter on the coast from British Columbia to Baja, while females go for the warmer coasts of Mexico and Central America.

Mudflats, lake and pond edges, especially along saline and alkaline waterbodies. Probes mudflats and shorelines for aquatic invertebrates; often feeds in standing water. Tightly contained flocks make precise maneuvers in unison.

Occasional spring migrant, April–May; common fall migrant, late June–mid-October, peaking in August. Absent in winter. Look for them at Gloyd Seeps Wetland, Potholes Reservoir, Bateman Island, Bennington Lake, Cold Springs NWR, Ladd Marsh WMA, Hatfield Lake, and Malheur and Lower Klamath NWRs.

Sharp, repeated *peeTpeeTpeeT* and individual *peeT*.

Least Sandpiper smaller with yellow-green legs. Semipalmated Sandpiper with shorter, straight bill.

Breeding adult.
All ages and sexes show yellow legs. Long, slightly upturned bill. Dark barring on neck and flanks heavier in breeding birds than nonbreeding and juveniles.

Nonbreeding adult.
Light barring on neck and flanks; upturned bill, yellow legs evident.

Breeding adult Lesser Yellowlegs.
Overall smaller than Greater Yellowlegs. Bill notably short and straight. Less barring than Greater.

GREATER YELLOWLEGS

Tringa melanoleuca

With breeding grounds spanning North America and dispersed migration routes, Greater Yellowlegs are widespread and common. Migrants turn up singly or in small groups in most waterbodies, feed on available food, and winter as far south as the tip of South America.

Marshes, mudflats, flooded agricultural fields. Forages in shallow water for aquatic invertebrates, fish, amphibians. Stabs, trolls, and sweeps bill using tactile sensors to catch prey. Finds prey by sight near surface; will chase down fish and swallow headfirst.

Common migrant March–May and July–November; less common in eastern Washington. Look for them at Saltese Flats, Rock and Soap Lakes, Hatton Coulee Rest Area, Sunnyside WRA, McKay Creek NWR, Haystack Reservoir, Adel Ponds, Summer Lake WA, and Wood River Wetland.

High-pitched *tu tu tu* regularly in a series of three.

Lesser Yellowlegs smaller, proportionally shorter bill, distinct call, *too-too.*

Breeding adult.
Yellow-orange bill with black tip. White orbital ring broken by black eyeline. Pale brown back and brown-spotted white breast. Often bobs tail.

Nonbreeding adult.
Pale brown back and incomplete breastband. Vertical white bar divides breastband from wing at shoulder. Relatively long tail, olive legs.

Adult Solitary Sandpiper.
Brown back with white spots; compare with brown back and black spots in Spotted Sandpiper. Throat and neck gray-brown; clean white breast and belly. Greenish legs versus Spotted's yellow-orange legs.

SPOTTED SANDPIPER

Actitis macularius

The small Spotted Sandpiper breeds in most freshwater habitats. Known for solitary habits, these sandpipers have continent-wide dispersal and are found on most quiet shorelines.

Freshwater habitat of all forms. Perpetually bobs tail. Unobtrusive hunter at water's edge, walks and wades. Pecks, probes, and hawks insects and other invertebrates. Flushes suddenly, often scolding as it does so. Shallow fluttery flight interspersed with glides.

Common breeder and migrant, April–October. Look for them at Turnbull NWR, Wilson Creek, Colfax Trail, Clover Island, Minam State RA, McKay Creek NWR, Cottonwood Canyon SP, Haystack Reservoir, Borax Lake, and Lake Ewauna Nature Trail.

Peet peet peet, *pee-peet pee-peet*, sometimes more liquid and slurred into a series.

Solitary Sandpiper found in similar habitat; distinguished from Spotted by larger size, gray back spotted with white, streaked breast, gray bill, yellow legs. Uncommon out of fall migration.

LENGTH: 7.5" / WINGSPAN: 15"

Adult.
Dark eyeline connects to long bill. Striped head. Back intricate pattern of black, white, and rust. Rust tail feathers. Fine barring on white breast and flanks. White belly. Yellow-green legs.

WILSON'S SNIPE

Gallinago delicata

Retiring shorebirds, Wilson's Snipes are more regularly seen in inland wetlands than at the beach. Fence posts are favorite springtime perches for males touching down after mating flight displays with high dives and singing tail feathers.

Marshes, wet meadows, and pastures. Probes in mud, shallow water, and along shorelines for invertebrates; stays near cover. Ground nester. Male and female split the chicks, each taking two to tend.

Year-round, locally common. Often seen displaying in spring; rarely seen otherwise. Look for them at Oakesdale Ponds, Potholes SP, Toppenish and McNary NWRs, Ladd Marsh WMA, Logan Valley, Crooked River Wetlands Complex, Malheur NWR, Catlow Valley Road, Hart Mountain, and Klamath WA.

Rising in intensity and volume *turka turka TUrkTUrk-TURKTURK*. Wind in tail feathers of displaying males creates ascending, then descending trembling winnow.

None on the East Side. More compact and burly than other shorebirds.

LENGTH: 10.5" / WINGSPAN: 18"

Breeding female. Gray cap. Long black bill connects to black eyestripe that expands and continues down the side of neck to shoulder. Rufous throat and breast. Gray-and-rust back. White belly and undertail coverts.

Adult nonbreeding. White face, throat, breast, belly, and undertail coverts. White eyebrow, gray eyestripe. Gray head, neck, and back. Black wingtips and tail. Long, straight black bill.

Male Red-necked Phalarope. Bill noticeably shorter and thicker than Wilson's. Gray cap, black face, rust stripe down the side of neck, rust throat. Breast gray. Back more evenly gray and rust.

Nonbreeding Red-necked Phalarope. Bright white face, neck, breast. Dark black eyestripe, white eyebrow. Dark back with white detail.

WILSON'S PHALAROPE

Phalaropus tricolor

Unlike the other phalaropes, Wilson's Phalaropes breed in the Intermountain West and fatten up for migration on saline lakes. In August, as many as 250,000 gather on Lake Abert in south-central Oregon.

Breeding habitat inland freshwater wetlands. Forages for invertebrates in shallow water; more often on shore than other phalaropes. Nests in dense vegetation close to wetlands. Fall staging occurs on shallow lakes, especially saline.

Common spring and fall migrant, April–early October. Look for them at Saltese Flats, Gloyd Seeps Wetland, Sunnyside WRA, Manns Pond, Ladd Marsh WMA, Fopiano Reservoir, Hatfield Lake, Malheur NWR, Borax Lake, Summer Lake WA, and Lake Ewauna Nature Trail.

Goose-like, repetitive *haunk haunk*, raspy clucking, and a hollow barking.

Red-necked Phalarope smaller with black head and red nape in breeding plumage. Nonbreeding Red-necks with black bill, black smudge through eye.

Nonbreeding adult.
Pale gray back, gray streaking on head, black wingtips visible at rest and in flight. Pale eye, no notable orbital ring. Breeding and nonbreeding adults with black ring on yellow bill, yellow legs. Breeding adult head pure white, orbital ring red.

Immature.
Tan streaking on head, scant on breast and secondaries. Tail and wingtips black. Pink bill with black ring including most of tip, pink legs.

Nonbreeding California Gull.
Larger than Ring-billed. Back and wings darker. Bill with red spot on lower mandible. Pale yellow-green legs.

RING-BILLED GULL

Larus delawarensis

You may be surprised by a gull in dry country, but Ring-billed Gulls are primarily an inland species in the West. Often associated with humans and towns, Ring-bills are the only gull breeding east of the Cascades.

Any waterbody, agricultural land, or fast-food parking lot. Opportunistic feeders; well adapted to humans and their eating habits. Colonial nester on sparse river islands and saline lakes and playas. Winter habitat along Columbia and Snake Rivers.

Common summer and locally common winter resident in eastern Washington; locally common summer resident in eastern Oregon. Look for them at Silver and Sheep Lakes, Scooteney Reservoir, Horn Rapids Dam, Umatilla NWR, Wallowa Lake SP, McKay Creek NWR, Crooked River Wetlands Complex, Antelope Reservoir, Lake Ewauna Nature Trail.

A long, classic gull screech followed by short, repetitive squawks.

Larger California Gull adult with red bill spot and pale legs.

LENGTH: 17.5" / WINGSPAN: 48"

Breeding adult. Somewhat elongated head sometimes appears wedge-shaped. Crisp black cap, brilliant red bill, dark wingtips in flight.

Immature. Similar to breeding adult but dark cap streaked, occasionally white on crown. Back and wings darker gray than adult, scalloped patterning.

Breeding adult Forster's Tern. Unlike Caspian Tern, bill never red, rather black or orange with black tip. Head rounder, less elongated. Black cap extends to back of neck.

Nonbreeding adult Forster's Tern. Significantly smaller than Caspian.

CASPIAN TERN

Hydroprogne caspia

The largest terns, Caspian Terns are powerful in the air with the grace and agility of a smaller tern. Like a pop-up event, breeding colonies can materialize rapidly in a season or two and just as rapidly disappear.

Freshwater shorelines, wetlands, rivers, lakes. Colonial nesters; colony locations shift with habitat availability and disturbance. Hunts on the wing from height, head down; hovers, plunge-dives for fish, submerging fully. Commonly swallows fish in the air.

Common summer resident April–September. Look for them at Silver Lake, Gloyd Seeps Wetland, Ginkgo Petrified Forest and Lyons Ferry SPs, Clover Island, Maryhill SP, Malheur NWR, Mann and Crump Lakes, Summer Lake WA, and Wood River Wetland.

Duck-like, raspy *quack* and screechy *rrraa rra rrraa rra*. Juvenile call peep-like.

Forster's Tern notably smaller and more delicate.

Adult.
Bare red head. Red facial skin contrasts with dark body and back, pale legs. Flight feathers silvery white against dark brown body. Appears unstable in flight. Neck typically retracted when perched, creating a hunched appearance.

Juvenile.
Brown head with pale band at neck. Flight feathers shimmery brown. Brown-black body, upper wings, and back.

TURKEY VULTURE

Cathartes aura

Dismissed as scavengers, Turkey Vultures are evolutionarily remarkable. Featherless heads prevent infectious buildup when birds are shoulder-deep in a carcass. Stomach acid strong enough to dissolve metal prevents disease despite their carrion diet.

Mixed undisturbed forest for nesting; open foraging grounds. Exquisite sense of smell; excellent vision. Solitary forager; gathers at carcasses. Roosts communally.

Common through summer and migration March–October. Look for them at Medical Lake, Steamboat Rock SP, Kamiak Butte CP, Ginkgo Petrified Forest SP, Biscuit Ridge Road, Willow Creek WA, Thief Valley Reservoir, Clarno boat ramp, Clyde Holliday State RA, Rock Creek Reservoir, Hart Mountain, and Gerber Reservoir.

Typically silent, an occasional hiss.

Northern Harrier (page 147) with similar lilting flight but stays close to ground; harrier's coloration, white rump distinct. Vultures wobble, maintain uplifted wing V (dihedral) not consistently seen in other soaring birds.

Adult.
Dark back. Dark eyestripe, crown of head white. When perched, wings extend to or beyond tail tip.

Adult.
Dark eyestripe and elbow patches. Breast pure white with faint collar. Long, narrow wings pointed at elbows.

OSPREY

Pandion haliaetus

A cosmopolitan species, Ospreys breed across the Northern Hemisphere. Once decimated by pesticides, its tolerance of humans and use of artificial nesting platforms allowed successful reestablishment of the population throughout its range.

Water. Expert fishers. Plunges feet first for fish near the surface. Ospreys readily adapted to nesting on power poles. Enormous stick nests used for multiple years.

Summer resident mid-March–early November; rarely overwinters. Look for them at Saltese Flats, Sun Lakes SP, Quincy WA, Burkett Lake RA, Wawawai CP, Horn Rapids Dam, Cottonwood Canyon SP, Trout Creek and Page Springs Campgrounds, and Putnam's Point.

High, fast, repetitive whistle. Less gull-like than Bald Eagle and often in a longer series.

Immature Bald Eagle (page 150) may have similar coloration but lacks white belly and is significantly larger.

Adult male.
White underwing with black wingtips and gray-black trailing edge. Gray head and back. White breast and belly speckled with brown; rump always white; feathers around eyes form facial disk reminiscent of owls.

Adult female.
Small bill and dark facial disk. Brown patterning on breast and wings. Dark brown back and upper wings; rump always white. Long tail broadly banded.

Adult Swainson's Hawk.
Rust-brown head and breast. Face white around bill and throat. Dark trailing wing broader than harrier. Dark tail.

NORTHERN HARRIER

Circus hudsonius

A denizen of open terrain, Northern Harriers are sexually dimorphic; brown females are 50 percent heavier than gray males. Habitat loss is the primary factor in an ongoing population decline.

Pastures, marshes, prairies. Hunts on the wing, pouncing on rodents, amphibians, and birds from above. Low flight unbalanced; birds tip side to side scanning, listening for prey. Often seen on fence posts. Partial migrant, moves to open hunting habitat; ground roosts communally in winter.

Common year-round resident and migrant. Look for them at Cheney Wetlands, Sun Lakes SP, Frenchman Coulee, Scooteney Reservoir, Palouse Falls SP, Biscuit Ridge Road, Umatilla NWR, Eureka Lane Marsh, Houston Lakes, Malheur NWR, and Wood River Wetland.

Call rapid series of *kek* or *quik* sounds.

Swainson's Hawk found in open grassland and agriculture. Harrier's uniform body coloration, long tail with white rump evident.

Adult.
Sexes similar but female notably larger. Red eye; charcoal-black cap, gray nape, dark gray back. Breast intricate rust-and-white barring, white undertail, white terminal tailband.

Juvenile.
Yellow eye; head and back streaked dark brown. Breast white with brown vertical streaks, white undertail.

Adult Sharp-shinned Hawk.
Smaller overall, rounder head than Cooper's. Proportionally shorter squared-off tail.

COOPER'S HAWK

Astur cooperii

Once persecuted as the marauding "chicken hawk" and nearly eradicated by the effects of DDT, Cooper's Hawks have readily adapted to human landscapes. Now common in urban parks and neighborhoods, Cooper's Hawks are precise fliers and masterful hunters.

Mixed woodland, riparian, and urban habitat. Hunts smaller birds by bursting into rapid flight from perch or on the wing; often hunts at bird feeders. Expert at maneuvering through dense trees. Less frequently pursues small mammals. Females notably larger than males.

Uncommon but widespread year-round resident and migrant. Look for them at Saltese Flats, Mountain View Cemetery, Gloyd Seeps Wetland, W. E. Johnson Park, Bennington Lake, Enterprise WMA, Smith Rock SP, Malheur NF, Page Springs Campground, Klamath Marsh NWR, and Klamath WA.

High, sharp *kikikikikikiki* in long series.

Sharp-shinned Hawk with round head and square-ended tail. Always smaller; Sharp-shinned female and Cooper's male not vastly different in size.

LENGTH: 16.5" / WINGSPAN: 31"

Adult.
Large size, massive bill, white head and tail definitive adult characteristics.

Immature.
Mottled white head and neck feathers make immature Bald Eagles look ratty and disheveled. Mottled brown with varying degrees of white or tan in underwing.

Adult Golden Eagle.
Dark brown with pale wing highlights. Golden mantle—back of head and nape. Bill proportional to head (note Bald's massive bill). Immature Golden often has white patterning in underwing like Bald's, but golden head always evident in both adults and juveniles; immature Golden with white tailband.

BALD EAGLE

Haliaeetus leucocephalus

The poster bird for the Endangered Species Act, depleted Bald Eagle populations struggled for survival in the 1960s. Rescued from bounties and DDT in the 1970s, they rebounded and now frequent much of eastern Washington and Oregon in winter. Although uncommon nesters on the East Side, Washington and Oregon now have 900 and 570 nesting pairs, respectively.

Lake and river shorelines; any large waterbody with fish. Opportunistic, actively hunts waterfowl, scavenges spawned-out salmon and roadkill and steals meals whenever possible.

Uncommon summer resident; locally common in winter. Look for them at Saltese Flats, Reardan Ponds, Coulee City Park, Potholes SP, Bennington Lake, Bateman Island, Smith Rock SP, Paulina Valley, Malheur NWR, Summer Lake WA, and Moore Park.

High, fluted whistle.

Immature Bald Eagles may resemble rare and declining Golden Eagles.

Light adult.
Light brown head, dark brown back; pale scapular feathers form a V. All adults with red tail except rare Harlan's subspecies.

Light adult.
Dark head, light breast with faint bellyband. Dark leading wing edge.

Ferruginous Hawk adult.
Noticeably larger than Red-tail. Body and underwing lighter. Tail white. Feathered legs make dark V against body.

Ferruginous Hawk adult.
Light-colored head, large bill. Uniform coloring of back unlike Red-tail's scapular V.

RED-TAILED HAWK

Buteo jamaicensis

The ubiquitous, generalist hawk of North America, Red-tailed Hawks benefit from human expansion and habitat alteration displacing other less-tolerant hawk species. Landscape changes from woodland to agriculture and open land favor this raptor.

Adaptable: wetlands, woodlands, grasslands, urban environments. Diet varies: small mammals, snakes, birds. Perches on any object above ground level and waits; also soars. Uses constant wing movement to hover; also kites, hanging motionless.

Very common year-round resident and migrant. Look for them at Iller Creek CA, Mountain View Cemetery, Gloyd Seeps Wetland, Palouse Falls SP, McKay Creek NWR, North Powder Pond, Woodward Marsh, Hatfield Lake, Fields Oasis, and Hagelstein Park.

High-pitched, raspy, descending scream. The sound of every bird of prey in movies, whether hawk, eagle, or vulture.

Uncommon Ferruginous Hawk with white tail feathers, rufous edges. Feathered legs coppery in adults, form V in flight.

LENGTH: 19" / WINGSPAN: 49"

Adult female.
White head, solid dark bellyband. Males overall darker, more patterning on head and throat, bellyband and breast more speckled.

Light adult female.
Dark wrist patches and wingtips, white tail with black subterminal band. Width of wings evenly broad for full length.

ROUGH-LEGGED HAWK

Buteo lagopus

The Arctic breeding, cliff-nesting Rough-legged Hawk is a common winter resident in the open country of the East Side. They show great variability in plumage, with light and dark birds. In the West, the light morph is more common, making identification easier.

Open landscapes. Hunts on the wing and often kites and hovers. Perches on telephone poles, fence posts, and the ground. Feeds primarily on rodents.

Common but widely scattered winter resident, October–March. Look for them at Saltese Flats, Davenport, Rocky Ford, McNary NWR, Hatfield Lake, North Powder Pond, Lawen Marshes, Summer Lake and Klamath WAs.

Typically silent. Alarm call piercing up note followed by descending scream.

Rough-legs and Red-tails (page 153) only common open country wintering raptors. White tail with dark subterminal band on Rough-leg definitive.

Male.
Gray cap, bold black vertical facial stripes. Back and tail rufous with scant barring. Tail with wide black terminal band and white tips. Wings slate-gray with black spots. Breast's rufous wash fading to white belly with black spotting.

Female.
Facial pattern less bold than male. Breast, belly, and underwing uniform white with rufous spotting sometimes blurring to mostly rufous. Back uniform rufous with black barring. Rufous tail with black tip.

Adult Merlin (Pacific subspecies).
Heavily streaked breast; mustache seen in other falcons barely visible. In flight, broad, pointy wings; faster flight than kestrel.

AMERICAN KESTREL

Falco sparverius

Although brightly colored American Kestrels are the only New World kestrel, their range spans North and South America and includes many subspecies. Easily identified as a falcon by its narrow, pointed wings; among the falcon family, kestrels are considered weak fliers.

Open country. Cavity nester; uses woodpecker holes, natural cavities, and nest boxes. Hunts from perches or on the wing; hovers. Catches invertebrates and small vertebrates, lizards, voles, songbirds with its feet.

Common year-round; moves from higher latitudes and elevations for winter. Look for them at Saltese Flats, Mountain View Cemetery, Columbia NWR, Horn Rapids CP, Rooks Park, Thief Valley Reservoir, Clarno Road, Smith Rock SP, Lawen Marshes, Fields Oasis, Hart Mountain, Silver Lake, and Klamath WA.

Kli kli kli kli kli, higher pitched, less burry than Northern Flicker.

Merlin with less distinctive facial markings; powerful, direct flight, primarily hunts birds.

Adult.
Lean and streamlined. Small, hooked bill; pronounced white eyebrow. Throat and breast white, small gray-brown spotting increases in size and frequency from breast to belly. Back gray with uniform patterning.

Adult.
Dark mustache faint in some individuals. Dark armpits are evident in flight.

Adult Peregrine Falcon.
Dark hood, full mustache. Heavier body.

Adult Peregrine Falcon.
Fine, uniform barring with no change in underwing color, more angular wings compared with Prairie Falcon.

PRAIRIE FALCON

Falco mexicanus

The unassuming Prairie Falcon easily flies below our bird-watching radar. Relatively nondescript compared to other falcons, it is nonetheless a fearless and precise predator. It is often seen in open desert and grasslands, making a beeline for some unknown destination or unseen prey.

Open country. Cliff nester. Prefers low desert and grassland vegetation. Feeds on ground squirrels during nesting season; grassland birds in winter. Agile in flight, direct, powerful with long approach to prey. Also perches and soars.

Fairly common year-round in eastern Oregon, less so in eastern Washington. Look for them at Steptoe Butte SP, Sprague Lake, Moses Coulee, Rattlesnake Mountain, Zumwalt Prairie, Smith Rock SP, Chickahominy Reservoir, Catlow Valley Road, Fort Rock SP, and Upper Klamath NWR.

Terse *qakqakqak* duck-like and repeated; also drawn out, rising, and repeated *qaaaak*.

Peregrine Falcon with bold mustache, uniform underwing pattern, pointier wings.

LENGTH: 16" / WINGSPAN: 40"

Male.
Grayer than female. In flight,
long tail tapers to a point,
tail feathers with white tips.

Female.
Rosy brown overall, paler than
male; black spots on wings.

Adult Eurasian Collared-Dove.
Black collar, red eye. Tan-gray with pink
wash, paler than Mourning Dove. Tail square
rather than tapered as in Mourning Dove.

Adult Rock Pigeon.
Typical pigeon with gray
body and black bars across
back. Head, neck, and breast
iridescent green, blue, gray.
Domesticated variations
include black, brown, and pied.

MOURNING DOVE

Zenaida macroura

One of the most widespread birds, calling Mourning Doves are commonly mistaken for owls. A short-lived species that can initiate nesting as often as every 30 days, they are the leading game bird in North America.

Open country, grasslands, residential areas. Feeds heavily on loose grain and weed seeds in agricultural landscapes. Some populations migrate but will remain as residents where food is available.

Widespread and common in summer; local in winter. Look for them at Philleo and Brook Lakes, Ione, Enterprise WMA, Condon City Park, Eagle Rock, Leslie Gulch, Chandler State Wayside, and Klamath WA.

Call *whoooo WHOO who who who*. Audible wing noise on takeoff, often accompanied by high *ti ti ti ti ti*.

Eurasian Collared-Dove with distinct band at back of neck. Rock Pigeon variable, typically gray rather than tawny, bulkier. Both tails rounded in flight.

Adult.
Large gray-brown facial disk, long ear tufts. Fine uniform patterning throughout body and back. Underwing pale.

Adult Long-eared Owl.
Rust-colored facial disk with black stripe through eyes creating deep V to bill. Much smaller, leaner than Great Horned.

GREAT HORNED OWL

Bubo virginianus

Adaptable and ubiquitous, Great Horned Owls are formidable predators. Named for their long, wide-set ear tufts, their acute sight, hearing, and neck rotation greater than 180 degrees leave nothing unnoticed. Including us.

Nocturnal hunters in most habitats. Typically hunts from a perch. Commonly visible at day roosts, in cottonwoods and shrubby thickets, draws, and wet areas. Uses nests abandoned by other species; will also use cliffs, buildings, and cavities, adding minimal lining material. Parents follow owlets as they grow and branch away from nest.

Common year-round. Look for them at Swanson Lakes WA, Central Ferry HMU, Fishhook Park, McNary and McKay Creek NWRs, Ladd Marsh WMA, Houston Lakes, Malheur NWR, Summer Lake WA, and Moore Park.

Classic owl hooting, *hoot hahoooo hooo hoo.*

Uncommon and often unseen Long-eared Owl shorter and slighter with upright ear tufts close together.

Male. Chunky when perched. Large head, oblong eye, white throat. White bar at front edge of wing and white wingbar obvious. Otherwise, cryptic coloration.

Male. White throatband, white wingbars, and white subterminal tail band. Female throatband muted, tailband lacking.

Adult Common Poorwill. Large eye, small bill. Cryptic mothlike gray back with undefined pattern. Underwing warm brown. Pale, narrow white throatband. Smaller than Common Nighthawk, with less constrained flight.

COMMON NIGHTHAWK

Chordeiles minor

One of the bird joys of summer mornings and evenings, these goatsuckers are agile, buoyant, and graceful. Well camouflaged but found across North America during breeding season. The indiscriminate use of pesticides and loss of nesting habitat threaten this species.

Open country and towns. Perches parallel to branches and commonly seen atop fence posts. Active at dawn and dusk, flies erratically, hawking insects from the air. Seemingly languid wing strokes provide remarkable power and speed; often glides. Roosts and nests on the ground, laying two eggs in a minimalist scrape.

Common in appropriate habitat, late May–mid-September. Look for them at Ginkgo Petrified Forest SP, Umtanum Creek, McNary NWR, Hatfield Lake, Thompson and Antelope Reservoirs, Fields Oasis.

Raspy, discreet *peent*. Male's wings create buzzy *vroooom* at bottom of mating dive.

Smaller Common Poorwill with shorter, rounder wings, lacks white wingbar. Nocturnal feeder. Calls distinct.

LENGTH: 9.5" / WINGSPAN: 24"

Male.
Slate-blue back and tail, white collar; dark slate head. Limited blue on flanks, no breastband and, unlike female, no rust on flanks or breast.

Female.
Same head and back as male with rust-color bellyband and flanks; necklace mottled rust and gray. Both male and female with massive bill, scruffy crest.

BELTED KINGFISHER

Megaceryle alcyon

As a scolding flash or a vigilant hunter, Belted Kingfishers haunt remote desert waters. Strong flight and the ability to hover and dive entirely underwater, emerging with a meal, make kingfishers enviable birds.

Open fresh water sufficient to sustain fish. Highly territorial, loyal to favorite perches. Streaks headfirst into shallow water, catching small fish in massive bill. Also hunts crayfish, amphibians, reptiles in shallow, sunlit waters. Solitary outside of breeding season; nests in burrows dug in sand and gravel banks. Will stay through winter if water remains open.

Year-round locally common resident. Look for them at Turnbull NWR, Potholes SP, Hood Park, Bennington Lake, Thief Valley Reservoir, Cottonwood Canyon SP, Ochoco Creek Trail, Malheur NWR, Ana Reservoir, and Hagelstein Park.

Distinct dry rattle freely given when disturbed from perch and regularly in flight. Often heard before seen.

Nothing similar in the desert.

LENGTH: 13" / WINGSPAN: 20"

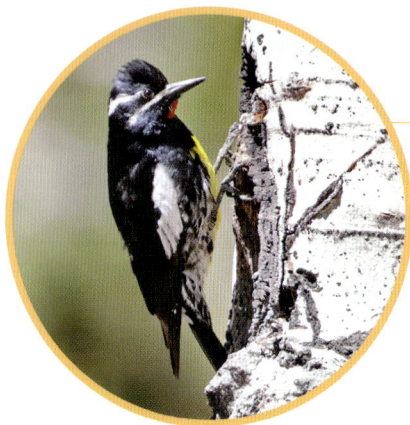

Male. Black head and back, red chin, white facial marks and white wingbar, bright yellow belly. Bold white rump evident in flight.

Female. Brown head and throat, black breastband, yellow belly. Black back with fine barring. Bold white rump evident in flight. No red on head or throat, no wingbars.

Row after row of sap wells is evidence that a Williamson's Sapsucker was here; listen for their drilling.

WILLIAMSON'S SAPSUCKER

Sphyrapicus thyroideus

Male and female Williamson's Sapsuckers appear as different species, not just different sexes. Both adults work to excavate the nest cavity in living trees and sometimes nap while clinging tree-side.

Larch, ponderosa pine, and mixed conifer–deciduous forests at elevation. Nests in conifer-dominant forests often with softwood component. Drills sap wells in neat vertical rows on conifer trees to feed on sap and insects. Ants important food source during nesting. Rarely overwinters.

Common breeder in eastern Cascades; rare in eastern Washington outside of Blue Mountains; common to uncommon in eastern Oregon, May to September. Look for them at Biscuit Ridge Road, Fields Spring SP, McCully Creek and Trail, Battle Mountain Forest SP, Steins Pillar Trailhead, Idlewild Campground, and Eagle Ridge/Shoalwater Bay.

Discreet rasping screeches *quEeeh*, somewhat Red-tailed Hawk–like; burry *raaAA*.

Largest sapsucker and unlike other woodpeckers.

Male.
Red forehead and crest, namesake red nape, red throat. White band across bill connects to shoulder and wraps to breast. Black-and-white patterning on back, white wingbars. Female similar with less red overall and white chin.

Female Red-breasted Sapsucker.
Mostly red head. Black wings and back with less white than other woodpeckers. White stripe below eye connects to white on back. White vertical stripe on wing. Male with bright red head, less white than female.

RED-NAPED SAPSUCKER

Sphyrapicus nuchalis

One of a three-species complex, Red-naped Sapsuckers were once lumped with Red-breasted and Yellow-bellied Sapsuckers. Elevated to independent species, the three regularly hybridize, providing intermediate characteristics and identification challenges.

Deciduous and mixed forest; ponderosa, aspen groves, riparian zones, and burns. Drills evenly spaced sap wells in trees; feeds on sap and insects it attracts. Hawks insects from air. Many other species feed from sap wells.

Relatively common summer resident. Look for them at Turnbull NWR, Mountain View Cemetery, Lewis Peak, Enterprise WMA, Big Summit Prairie, Steens and Hart Mountains, and Summer Lake WA.

Piercing, deliberate shriek, *weer weer weer*; drums in series of fast and then slow taps.

Red-breasted Sapsucker rare off eastern Cascade slopes—red head, throat, and breast, less black-and-white patterning. Yellow-bellied Sapsucker rare in eastern Washington and Oregon.

Adult.
Dark head, red face, gray
breast and collar, pink belly—all
unique among woodpeckers.

LEWIS'S WOODPECKER

Melanerpes lewis

A federal species of concern and Oregon sensitive species, Lewis's Woodpecker is not your average woodpecker. Often flying in straight lines, with no undulations, they also zigzag in pursuit of insects, which they hawk from the air. Loosely colonial, birds rarely excavate nest holes and commonly reuse cavities.

Breeds in open pine forests, cottonwood-dominated riparian woods, and selectively logged or burned pine stands with standing dead trees. In winter, oak forests (or stands of other mast-producing trees) and orchards for acorns. Stores acorns and seeds in tree crevices for winter.

Common but local breeder. Look for them at Ephrata Cemetery, Lyons Ferry SP, Bennington Lake, Oak Springs Hatchery, Catherine Creek SP, Page Springs Campground, Klamath Marsh NWR, and Moore Park.

Churr churr churr. Variable calls: woodpecker *pik*, jay-like screeches, and high-pitched nuthatch-like chatter.

None. Flight and glide can appear jay- or crow-like.

Male.
Heavy black eyestripe connects to red dot at back of head. Clean white breast. Black wings with white spots. Stiff tail feathers used for bracing on tree trunks.

Female.
White back and white spotting on wings. No red. Both sexes have small bill with tuft of bristles at nasal opening.

Hairy Woodpecker male.
White back in both sexes and red spot at back of male's head same as Downy. Heavier, longer bill, and proportionally larger body.

Hairy Woodpecker female.
Overall larger than Downy, less white spotting on wings. Downy male and Hairy female can overlap in bill size; red head marking on Downy male can help distinguish the two.

DOWNY WOODPECKER

Dryobates pubescens

North America's smallest woodpecker and one of the most common, Downy Woodpeckers are well distributed across the continent. Birds may move laterally into available winter habitats but do not appear to migrate.

Mostly lower elevation and riparian areas; also found in urban areas. Downies feed on insects and seeds gleaned from trees and woody stems of flowering plants and shrubs and enjoy suet at backyard feeders. Excavates nest hole in dead limbs and trees.

Common year-round resident in appropriate habitat. Look for them at Granite Lake, Gloyd Seeps Wetland, Lyons Ferry SP, Biscuit Ridge Road, Sunnyside WRA, Smith Rock SP, Clyde Holliday State RA, Idlewild Campground, Goose Lake State RA, and Wood River Wetland.

Call note sharp *pik*. Rattling series of rapid, even, descending *pikpikpik*. Rapid drumming.

Hairy Woodpecker notably larger; no barring on outer tail feathers. Prefers mature, open forest.

Male.
All-white head with red spot at back. All-black body, white wing edge.

Female.
All-white head lacks red spot. All-black body, white wing edge. Underwing mottled white and black in flight.

WHITE-HEADED WOODPECKER

Dryobates albolarvatus

Like many woodpeckers, White-headed Woodpeckers rely on dead trees and snags for feeding and nesting. Already restricted to a narrow range from British Columbia to Southern California, forestry practices, including snag removal, fire suppression, and even-aged stands, are detrimental to this federal species of concern and Oregon sensitive species.

Primarily found in ponderosa pine forests, even when burned or logged. Typical woodpecker flight. Feeds on invertebrates gleaned from bark, crevices, and snags, and pine seeds extracted from cones. Territorial cavity nester.

Uncommon year-round forest resident of eastern Cascades and central and northeastern Oregon. Look for them at Umptanum Road, Morgan Lake, relatively widespread in Ochoco, Malheur, and Fremont-Winema NFs, Klamath Marsh NWR, and Klamath Ridge View Trail.

Sharp *piki piki* in quick succession. Rattle call higher pitched than flicker.

None with distinct white head.

LENGTH: 9.25" / WINGSPAN: 16"

Male.
Brown crown and gray face with red mustache. Spotted breast, black bib, reddish orange tail.

Female.
Brown crown and brown around eye, face gray, black bib. No red mustache. In flight, male and female show distinct reddish underwing and a white rump.

NORTHERN FLICKER

Colaptes auratus

Once two species, the Red-shafted Flicker and the Yellow-shafted Flicker were merged into the Northern Flicker. The less charismatic name doesn't stop the Northwest's most common woodpecker from pounding on signs and stovepipes.

Mixed open woodland, parks, and urban neighborhoods; needs large trees for nesting. Excavates nest cavities but primarily feeds on the ground for ants; also eats fruits in season. Like most woodpeckers, uses tail to brace on tree trunks and has undulating flight.

Common year-round resident. Yellow-shafted migrants join resident Red-shafted population in winter. Look for them at Iller Creek CA, Sun Lakes and Ginkgo Petrified Forest SPs, Lost Island HMU, Mecca Flats, Haystack Reservoir, Ochoco Creek Trail, Leslie Gulch, Fields Oasis, Fort Rock SP, and Putnam's Point.

Several calls: lengthy, rapid, even *wikwikwikwikwik*, often with stutter start; slower, repeated *weeka weeka weeka*; and sharp *kleer*.

Nothing else looks like a flicker.

Male. Red forehead, crest, and mustache. White eyebrow, black eyeline. All-black breast.

Female. Gray forehead, red crest, black eyestripe, thin white eyebrow. Long, heavy bill. All-black back.

PILEATED WOODPECKER

Dryocopus pileatus

The largest remaining woodpecker species in North America, Pileated Woodpeckers are dependent on mature forests with large dead and dying trees. The uniquely oval-shaped holes these woodpeckers create and use for feeding, nesting, and roosting cavities support a myriad of secondary uses for other species.

Mature forests with large dead and dying trees and snags. Feeds primarily on ants and beetle larvae excavated from rotting trees. Typical woodpecker tree-climbing and tail-propping behavior.

Locally common year-round resident in suitable habitat. Look for them at Iller Creek CA, Lewis & Clark Trail SP, Whitman Mission National Historic Site, Emigrant Springs SP, Shelton Wayside CP, Idlewild Campground, Moore Park, and Eagle Ridge/Shoalwater Bay.

Similar to Northern Flicker (page 179), higher pitched and slower *wikwikwikwikwik*. Drumming starts rapidly, tapers off toward end.

None. Large size unique among western woodpeckers.

Adult.
White or bluish vertical stripes on forehead. Grayish black head and prominent crest, grayish black throat and bill. Shimmering blue breast. Grayish neck and upper back; deep blue wings and tail with fine barring.

STELLER'S JAY

Cyanocitta stelleri

Adhering to a curious form of territoriality, long-term Steller's Jay pairs are dominant at their nest; increased distance from the nest decreases social dominance. This creates a shifting mosaic of social interactions based on relative position to the home nest and surrounding breeding pairs.

Fragmented conifer forests and edges, woodlands, urban areas, river bottoms. Omnivorous, raucous, and quick to flee disturbance. Feeds while walking on ground; readily visits bird feeders, campgrounds, picnic areas.

Common year-round resident in forested habitat. Look for them at Fields Spring SP, Bennington Lake, lower Biscuit Ridge Road, Minam State RA, Morgan Lake, Battle Mountain Forest SP, Delintment Lake, Page Springs Campground, and Collier Memorial SP.

Highly variable but always jay-like. Raspy, scolding chatter; high-pitched squeaks; rattles and squeals.

California Scrub-Jays (page 185) have white breast and belly, blue head, lack crest.

Adult.
Black bill and wedge through eye; thin white eyebrow. Bright blue head, wings, and tail; gray back.

Adult.
White throat and belly; indistinct blue-gray neckband.

CALIFORNIA SCRUB-JAY

Aphelocoma californica

Smart, sassy, and noticeable, California Scrub-Jays are found at lower elevations and more exclusively in urban areas than other corvids. When not hanging out at the local feeder, scrub-jays depend on acorns and pine seeds for winter survival, and an individual can cache as many as 5,000 acorns a season.

Shrubby habitat, open oak and pine forest. Drier and more urban sites than Steller's Jay. Less sociable than Steller's. Nonmigratory and territorial. Omnivorous; feeds while hopping on ground and in low branches.

Year-round resident; common in appropriate habitat. Look for them at Yakima Area Arboretum, Prosser Dam, Touchet, Joseph, Maupin City Park, Smith Rock SP, John Day, Moore Park, Frenchglen, Lakeview Cemetery.

Screeet screeet. Variable; higher pitched and less raspy than Steller's Jay (page 183).

Steller's Jay (page 183) with black head, throat, and crest; remainder blue.

Adult.
Plumage appears sleek.
Black head and bib. White
belly, long black legs.
Iridescent blue-green
wings. Long blue-black tail.

Adult.
Heavy black bill. White shoulder.
In flight, white under- and upper-
wing patches. Black wingtips.

BLACK-BILLED MAGPIE

Pica hudsonia

Loved and hated, Black-billed Magpies are undeniably impressive. Flashy and gregarious birds, they outsmart us regularly and rarely let a predator pass without comment. Magpies build massive, enclosed stick nests with mud floors that are sometimes reused by Long-eared Owls.

Nests primarily in dense riparian vegetation; more broadly distributed out of breeding season. Found at lower elevations in towns, ranches, roadsides, and sagebrush steppe. Opportunistic in feeding. Walks and hops. Agile in flight. Talkative.

Common year-round resident. Look for them at Turnbull NWR, Northrup Canyon, Potholes SP, Central Ferry HMU, Rock Creek Park, John Day Fossil Beds NM, Forest Conservation Area (Prairie City), Catlow Valley Road, Nuss Lake.

Scolding, chattering, repeated *chack chack chack*; often single *ack*.

None. Large size, iridescence, bold pattern, long tail, with corvid attitude unique.

Adult.
Pale gray face with faint white around eye and forehead. Body gray. Wings black with white trailing edge of secondaries visible perched and in flight. White undertail coverts. Black tail with white outer tail feathers.

CLARK'S NUTCRACKER

Nucifraga columbiana

A denizen of high mountain lakes and open forests, Clark's Nutcracker is closely associated with whitebark, piñon, and limber pines. Nutcrackers can carry dozens of seeds under their tongues and are the primary seed dispersers for several pine species.

Found at tree line in summer, lower in winter. Specializes in opening conifer cones, caching thousands of seeds a season. Both sexes incubate eggs, allowing females to retrieve stashed seeds.

Common year-round in the right habitat. Occasional along eastern Cascade front from Ellensburg to Lakeview; mostly absent in open sagebrush plains of eastern Washington and Oregon, but regular in Umatilla, Malheur, Ochoco, and Fremont-Winema NFs, Wallowa Mountains.

Vocal. Raspy, harsh *reah reah reah*. Wing *whoop* often heard before calls.

Nutcracker's large size and long bill distinguish it from Northern and Loggerhead Shrikes (page 223).

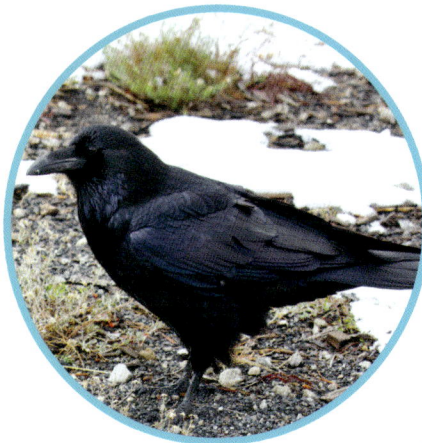

Adult.
Large size. Long wings extend at least the length of the tail. All shimmery black.

Adult.
Long, heavy bill with nasal bristles, bristly throat.

Adult American Crow.
Uniformly glossy black, big head and bill relative to body size. Tail squarish. Wing-tips do not extend to the length of the tail, as in ravens, and crows never soar.

COMMON RAVEN

Corvus corax

From creator of the universe to trickster and bad omen, Common Ravens are vividly represented in mythology and everyday life. The largest songbird, and distributed across the Northern Hemisphere, their well-deserved reputation is that of intelligence, adaptability, and skill.

Open country from mountains and coast to sagebrush and desert. Omnivorous and opportunistic. Feeds on carrion, eggs, chicks, rodents, insects, and grains. Commonly soars; unparalleled in-flight barrel rolls.

Common year-round resident. Look for them at West Plains, Northrup Canyon, Quincy WA, Hat Rock SP, Zumwalt Prairie, Ochoco Lake CP, Malheur NWR, Catlow Valley Road, and Hart Mountain.

Varied and extensive, from hoarse *caws* and *ghokk*s to deep chortles and gurgling bubbles.

Short tail, broad wings distinguish American Crow from larger raven. Crows never soar and often mob ravens.

LENGTH: 24" / WINGSPAN: 53"

Male.
Full, iridescent gorget, variable red head; appears black in certain lighting. Pale eyering continues down neck. Green back, gray breast with greenish flanks.

Female.
Faint white eyebrow. Gray breast, sometimes small throat spot. Greenish back, broad tail with white-tipped feathers.

Black-chinned Hummingbird male.
Black chin with purple iridescent band above pale breast. Head may look black. Green back, green wash on breast.

Black-chinned Hummingbird female.
Head more gray than Anna's. When perched, wings at least length of tail, may project beyond.

ANNA'S HUMMINGBIRD

Calypte anna

The Anna's Hummingbird's range has expanded north in the last 50 years. Taking advantage of urban gardens and feeders, these territorial birds stake claims and don't budge.

Urban areas with native and exotic landscaping species and winter-blooming plants. Breeding often begins in late winter. Female responsible for nesting and chick-rearing. Males provide aggressive displays and fierce territorial defense.

Locally common resident. Uncommon in open landscapes. Look for them at Pullman, Porter's Pond, Walla Walla, Crooked River Campground, Summer Lake WA, and Moore Park.

Buzzy, insect-like rasp. Call simple *tchip*, more mechanical than similar sparrow calls. Mating display dive ends with a chirpy pop, like clicking your tongue.

Black-chinned male has white upper breast; female lacks chin marking. Female and juvenile Rufous Hummingbirds (page 195) with pale rufous sides and undertail, rusty base to tail feathers.

Male.
Rufous head, back, and body. Shimmering orange throat with white band fading into rufous breast and belly. Dark green wings. When fanned, tail serrated, rufous with black tips.

Female.
Brownish green back and head, rufous sides and base of tail. Throat with central red spot in good light.

Calliope Hummingbird male.
Gorget rosy, streaked. No rufous. Green back, breast with green wash. Unlike Rufous, tail short, rounded when fanned. Wingtips slightly longer than tail when perched.

RUFOUS HUMMINGBIRD

Selasphorus rufus

A zippy hummingbird with a big presence, this early-season breeder relies on spring-blooming flowers for mating and nesting. By midsummer, it moves to the mountains to fatten up on alpine flower nectar for migration.

Brushy coniferous forest and regrowth, edges, meadows. Aggressively territorial. Female entirely responsible for incubation and chick-rearing. Does not overwinter north of Mexico.

Common summer resident. Arrives February–March; gone in August. Look for them at Turnbull NWR, Patrick Park, Potholes SP, Chamna Natural Preserve, Union County Fairgrounds, Wallowa Mountains, Smith Rock SP, Steens Mountain, and Moore Park.

Sharp *tchip* and raspy squeaks. Displaying males create loud squawks as air moves through outer wing feathers.

Calliope and Anna's Hummingbirds (page 193) have no rufous; females and juveniles of several species overlap in appearance and are difficult to distinguish. Calliope males with streaked magenta throat, green head.

LENGTH: 3.75" / WINGSPAN: 4.5"

Male.
Black-and-white facial
marking most notable.
Black horns usually evident.
Throat pale yellow, banded
by black above white breast
and belly. Back with fine patterning in warm brick brown.
Outer tail feathers black,
with narrow white trim.

Female.
Similar facial pattern to male
but muted, less conspicuous; no
horns. Throat paler yellow. Dark
brown breastband. Tail like male's.

HORNED LARK

Eremophila alpestris

A small bird with a big range, Horned Larks nest across North America and Asia north to the Arctic Ocean and from sea level to 13,000 feet. Equally at home in tundra and alpine zones, there are 21 subspecies in North America that fill every open-country niche.

Sparsely vegetated landscapes, sage, shrub-steppe, desert, agriculture. Ground dweller; often runs before flying. Adults feed mostly on seeds, but insects are important food for young. Some populations resident; winter flocks often northern migrants.

Common year-round resident. Look for them at Reardan Ponds, Swanson Lakes WA, Washtucna, Rattlesnake Mountain, Virtue Flat, Fort Rock Road, Christmas Valley, Pete French Round Barn SP, Lower Klamath NWR.

High, sweet, jumbled notes. High, thin notes, *tsi tsi.*

Nothing similar or with the same penchant for playing chicken with cars.

Adult.
Pale with buff or white throat, breast gradually darkening toward tail. Wings more curved than White-throated Swift and bow-shaped when fully open. Adult and juvenile similar. Shallow, fluttering wingbeats; rapid flight.

During migration, Vaux's Swifts roost by the thousands in old chimneys.

Adult White-throated Swift.
Conspicuous white throat and belly. White patches on flanks where wing meets rump.

VAUX'S SWIFT

Chaetura vauxi

Fast and nimble with stiff wingbeats, Vaux's Swifts are superb fliers. Ongoing loss of forest habitat, old chimneys, and insect populations makes these aerial insectivores, the smallest North American swift, vulnerable.

Forests and leafy towns. Historically roosted and nested in old-growth forest snags and hollow tree trunks; now adapted to human structures. Lives entirely on airborne insects caught on the wing.

Fairly common summer resident April to mid-September; congregates in flocks of thousands during fall migration. Look for them feeding in the air over Saltese Flats, Bateman Island, Bennington Lake, Biscuit Ridge Road, Emigrant Springs SP, North Powder Pond, Hatfield Lake, Summer Lake WA, and Moore Park.

Rapid, persistent, high-pitched chipping, often with a trill or rolled *R*.

Larger White-throated Swift with longer wings and tail; tail notched.

LENGTH: 4.75" / WINGSPAN: 12"

Male.
Metallic blue head and back with hints of green; appears dark blue or black in some lights. Throat and breast white; distinct division between cheek and throat. Wings blue with gray edges and tips. Tail gray, with shallow notch.

Female.
Gray-brown back and wings, with green shimmer. Shows same distinct contrast between cheek and throat as male. Juvenile similar with gray-brown breastband.

Violet-green Swallow male.
Vivid green head, back, shoulders. Bright white cheeks, throat, and breast. White extends around rump, not quite creating a solid band; divides green back from violet tail. Dark primaries. Female with pale brown head, back less brilliant green, almost no visible violet. Narrower wings than Tree.

TREE SWALLOW

Tachycineta bicolor

Unexpectedly, Tree Swallows prefer open landscapes for hunting and only retreat to the trees for nesting. Often seen hunting over open water, they dip to drink as they fly. Despite their adaptability, the loss of forest habitat and the decline of insects make their future a troubling prospect.

Open landscapes, especially near water. Aerial insectivore. Nests in abandoned woodpecker holes, bluebird boxes, and human structures. Commonly flocks with other swallows.

Common breeder and migrant late February/March to September. Look for them at Cheney Wetlands, Swanson Lakes and Quincy WAs, Horn Rapids CP, Deschutes River State RA, Smith Rock SP, Davis Creek Park, Malheur NWR, Hart Mountain, and Klamath WA.

High, oft-repeated chatter with liquid bubbles. Call *chi chi chi-uh*.

Violet-green Swallows marginally smaller, shimmery green, white on flanks extends around to rump.

LENGTH: 5.75" / WINGSPAN: 14.5"

Adult.
Buffy white forehead and breast; pale collar, gray wings. Blue-black cap and wings. Dark rust-red throat. Light rufous rump.

Adult Bank Swallows.
Uniform gray-brown back, wings, tail. White throat extends around shoulders but does not meet at back of neck. White breast, gray-brown band between throat and breast. Shallow but sharp tail notch, unlike Cliff's square tail.

CLIFF SWALLOW

Petrochelidon pyrrhonota

Cliff Swallows are finely skilled craftsbirds, collecting mud by the mouthful to build gourd-shaped nests under cliffs, bridges, and eaves. The extensive American highway infrastructure allowed this species to expand well beyond its original western boundary.

Open country, typically near water. Aerial insectivores; expert fliers. Colonial nesters, with colonies of a few pairs or hundreds.

Common summer resident late March to September. Look for them at Riverfront Park, Sheep Lake, Potholes SP, Getty's Cove, Sunnyside WRA, Maupin City Park, Ochoco Reservoir, Silvies Valley, Pete French Round Barn SP, Fields Oasis, Lake Abert, and Hagelstein Park.

R2-D2 on speed. Calls *churr*s, stutters, burry chatter. Lower than Barn Swallow (page 205).

Bank Swallows with pale brown breastband and white throat; lack blue head, rust cheeks, pale forehead and rump.

Male.
Buff-orange belly,
rust-colored throat and
forehead; shimmery
blue back and head.
Long forked tail.

**Adult Northern
Rough-winged Swallow.**
Uniformly brown above, clean
white or pale buff throat, breast,
and belly. No distinction between
male and female; juveniles with
pale rusty wingbars. In flight,
uniform color; short, squared
tail evident.

BARN SWALLOW

Hirundo rustica

The cosmopolitan Barn Swallow ranges on all continents except Antarctica. Widespread and well adapted to humans, it, like many aerial insectivores, is undergoing a significant population decline. Agricultural chemicals, especially neonicotinoids, are suspected.

Open landscapes with water sources. Builds mud nests on eaves, bridges, and in barns on both vertical and horizontal surfaces under protective roofing. Highly maneuverable, feisty, rambunctious flight. Drinks on the wing.

Common breeder April–September. Look for them at Saltese Flats, Silver Lake, Swanson Lakes WA, Moses Lake, Sentinel Bluffs, Rock Creek and Dufur City Parks, Rhinehart Canyon, Morgan Lake, Fossil, Prineville Reservoir, Hotel Diamond, Hart Mountain, and Lake Ewauna Nature Trail.

Nonstop squeaky chatter mixed with trills and chips. Higher pitched than Cliff Swallow (page 203).

Nothing else with long tail feathers and aerial ability. All tan and buff Northern Rough-winged is smaller and lacks color.

Adult.
Tiny black bill, black cap and throat; buff to faint chestnut flanks. White stripe expanding from bill, across cheek, to shoulder.

Adult Chestnut-backed Chickadee.
Heathered black cap, deep chestnut back and flanks compared with black cap and gray back of Black-capped Chickadee.

Adult Mountain Chickadee.
White eyebrow unique to Mountain. Pale breast and belly, more uniformly gray-white than Black-capped. Back and tail evenly gray.

BLACK-CAPPED CHICKADEE

Poecile atricapillus

From the Pacific to the Atlantic, Black-capped Chickadees are a cheery, sturdy species. Able to enter a state of regulated hypothermia, they endure the deepest cold by dropping their body temperature by as much as 50 degrees F.

Deciduous and mixed deciduous-conifer forest, open woodlands, river bottomlands, leafy urban areas. Vocal, curious; often hangs upside down to glean insects, seeds from bark. Gathers in mixed winter flocks.

Common year-round resident. Largely absent from Columbia Basin and central Oregon. Look for them at Dishman Hills Natural Area, Mountain View Cemetery, Horn Rapids CP, Magpie Forest, Bennington Lake, Minam State RA, Thief Valley Reservoir, Idlewild Campground, and Putnam's Point.

Classic, quintessential *chick-a-dee dee dee*.

Higher elevation Chestnut-backed Chickadee with gray cap, namesake dark chestnut back; found in wet, dense forest. Mountain Chickadee with white eyebrow common in drier, more open forests.

Adult.
Buffy olive wings and back, white wingbar, pale throat and breast. Partial eyering, uniform gray head. Notched tail.

Adult male.
Slightest hint of ruby crown, which is not often shown.

Female Bushtit.
Male and female with brown head, gray overall, long tailed. Female with pale eye. Male and fledglings with dark brown eyes.

Male Golden-crowned Kinglet.
Black-bordered golden crown visible; male crown yellow and orange when raised. Back more yellow-green than Ruby-crowned. Black eyestripe with white eyebrow. Female with tannish gray breast and belly.

RUBY-CROWNED KINGLET

Corthylio calendula

Commonly heard high in the canopy, Ruby-crowned Kinglets rarely show their ruby crowns unless agitated. Often found in mixed-species flocks with Golden-crowned Kinglets, chickadees, nuthatches, and creepers.

Breeds in coniferous forests; winters in conifers, mixed woodlands, and brushy habitat. Gleans insects and eggs from foliage; sometimes hovers. Calls insistently and flicks its wings incessantly.

Uncommon year-round resident. Winters in Columbia Basin and southeastern Oregon; summers in surrounding mountains. Look for them at Turnbull NWR, Patrick Park, Sentinel Bluffs, Bateman Island, Lewis Peak, Wallowa Lake SP, Clyde Holliday State RA, Malheur NWR, Page Springs Campground, and Goose Lake State RA.

Mixed high, clear whistles and burry repeated *cheeta*. Also, tiny, sharp *tsip*.

Golden-crowned Kinglet with black-and-gold striped cap and white eyebrows. Bushtits marginally larger, all gray, no eyering.

Adult.
White breast and throat, gray cheeks and head. White ring incomplete but extends across bill to connect eyes. Olive-gray back, wings, and flanks.

Adult Warbling Vireo.
Pale overall, gray back, white throat and breast. Flanks and wings with faint olive wash. Pale eyebrow. Less bold colors than Cassin's.

CASSIN'S VIREO

Vireo cassinii

Often well hidden in the canopy, Cassin's Vireos hold true to the genus trait of repetitive singing. The tireless song may lead you to a glimpse of one foraging among the branches.

Dry, mid-elevation mixed forest with shrubby understory; more common in Douglas fir than ponderosa pine. Also uses riparian areas. Gleans foliage for insects, also hawks and hovers.

Fairly common late April to early October. Look for them at Iller Creek CA, Oasis Park (Ephrata), W. E. Johnson Park, Biscuit Ridge Road, Wallowa Lake and Red Bridge SPs, Idlewild Campground, Malheur NWR, Fields Oasis, and Moore Park.

Variations on *cheerl*, *cheeri*, *cheer*. Repetitious and tenacious. Burry chatter when disturbed.

Warbling Vireo pale beige with little color and faint white eyebrow. More common in riparian trees, cottonwoods, and aspens.

Adult. Proportionally large head with barely noticeable crest. Dark head and back, pale throat. Gray flanks encroach toward center of white breast.

Adult Western Wood-Pewee. Smaller than Olive-sided, distinct wingbars. Breast gray; belly and flanks more extensively white than Olive-sided.

OLIVE-SIDED FLYCATCHER

Contopus cooperi

A federal species of concern, Olive-sided Flycatcher populations are in significant decline across North America. This species traditionally relied on post-fire habitat for breeding, and while nesting increased in harvested forests of the Pacific Northwest, superficially similar cut forest may not provide the necessary components for successful reproduction.

Coniferous forest with openings, including wetlands, meadows, and burn edges. Chooses high, exposed perches; hawks insects from air. Aggressively defends nest. Extremely agile when in pursuit of insect quarry.

Common May–September. Look for them at Iller Creek CA; Steptoe Butte, Potholes, and Fields Spring SPs, Bateman Island, Hatfield Lake, Idlewild and Page Springs Campgrounds, and Moore Park.

One of the most recognizable flycatcher calls, often stated as *quick THREE beers*.

Western Wood-Pewee distinguished by gray wingbars, proportionally longer tail, smaller bill, pale gray breast, and yellow belly wash.

Adult.
Dark upper mandible, yellow-orange lower; full eyering more pronounced at back; slight crest; tail extends well beyond wing primaries.

Adult Willow Flycatcher.
Olive-brown back with pale wingbars. Grayish brown head. Broad bill, dark above, yellow-orange below. Wings project beyond body at rest. Pale buffy throat, breast, and undertail. Less olive than Western.

WESTERN FLYCATCHER

Empidonax difficilis

One of the endlessly difficult *Empidonax* flycatchers, the inland and coastal versions of Western Flycatchers were divided into two species in the 1980s (Pacific-Slope and Cordilleran) and rejoined in 2023. This is good news for those of us who already struggle to separate the many seemingly identical flycatchers.

Dense, shady forest, floodplains, riparian zones. Late spring migrant. Flicks tail when perched. Low canopy forager hawks and gleans insects. Nest sites include tree forks, cavities, and bark, cliff shelves with overhead shelter.

Common breeder May–September. Look and listen for them at Liberty Lake CP, Turnbull NWR, Potholes and Lyons Ferry SPs, Bennington Lake, Hilgard Junction SP, Malheur NWR, Fields Oasis, and Wood River Wetland.

Three-part song in succession: high whistled *tsip*; thin, lispy *teeWEET*; final sharp *piT*.

Willow Flycatcher best distinguished by habitat (wet and brushy) and song (buzzy, burry, repeated *FITZbew*).

Adult.
Dark gray head, back, and tail. Slight
crest. Pale gray throat and breast. Pale
rufous belly, the color of sandstone.

SAY'S PHOEBE

Sayornis saya

An understated bird, the Say's Phoebe's muted colors and calm manner endear it to many. Its habit of nesting on porch lights and over doorways, not so much. However, it graciously allows humans passage without much ado.

Open sagebrush, canyons, grasslands. Hunts from low perch, flower stalks, and shrub branches; hawks insects from the air. Frequently nests on buildings, under eaves and porches.

Fairly common February–October; occasionally over-winters. Look for them at Saltese Flats, West Medical Lake, Wilson Creek, Columbia NWR, Willow Creek WA, Pendleton River Parkway, Ukiah, John Day Fossil Beds NM, Houston Lakes, Jordan and Christmas Valleys, and Klamath WA.

Sweet whistle *peeEww* rises before tapering off. Sometimes a burry *prrrt*. Can be repetitive and insistent with calls.

None in this stretch of sagebrush.

Adult.
Puffy gray crest. Grayish white throat and breast, pale yellow wash on belly and undertail coverts. Wingbars, rufous primaries.

Adult.
Often seen puffed and fluffed in the wind. Strong black bill conical. Long tail rufous with dark terminal edge.

ASH-THROATED FLYCATCHER

Myiarchus cinerascens

Among flycatchers, this species stands out. Larger and more colorful, it often sits quietly, scanning its surroundings. If no prey is apparent, it moves to a new perch a short distance away.

Dry shrub scrub, riparian woodland, open forest. Cavity nester; will use nest boxes. Forages for invertebrates and small lizards in foliage and on ground, moving regularly to new perch. Hovers while hunting; flutters between perches.

Uncommon May–August. Nearly absent from Columbia River east in Washington and northeast Oregon. Look for them at Rock Creek Park, Deschutes River State RA, Cottonwood Canyon SP, Priest Hole, Smith Rock SP, Hatfield Lake, North Shore Road (Prineville), Beulah Reservoir, Malheur NWR, Fields Oasis, Fort Rock SP, and Summer Lake WA.

Repeated *qibiRri qibiRri*, sometimes burry. Call *kribit* or *brriT*.

None. Large size, puffy crest, long tail unique among area flycatchers.

Adult.
Pale gray head. White
throat and breast,
yellow belly. Gray back
with green wash, brown
wings, dark tail with
white outer feathers.

Adult Eastern Kingbird.
Bright white throat, pale
gray breastband, white belly.
Charcoal-gray head darker
than Western. Brown wings.
Black tail with white tip.

WESTERN KINGBIRD

Tyrannus verticalis

Western Kingbirds are quintessential open-country flycatchers. Visible anywhere with available perches and a scattering of trees for nesting, they are vocal and fearless.

Open country with trees, shrubs, or utility poles for nest sites. Commonly perches on and hunts from power lines and fences. Hawks insects and drops from perch to take prey from ground. Fiercely defends nest; mobs hawks and ravens.

Common April–mid-September. Look for them at Saltese Flats, Potholes SP, Vernita Bridge, Fields Spring SP, Corral Ditch (Baker City), John Day Fossil Beds NM, Crooked River Wetlands Complex, Hatfield Lake, Beulah Reservoir, Pete French Round Barn SP, and Klamath WA.

String of high-pitched, flat, squeaky syllables suddenly rising as if the bird was goosed, *tip tip tip tip TiTIPti*.

Eastern Kingbird more slender, with narrower bill, lacks bold yellow belly.

Adult.
Stout hooked bill. Black eye mask connects across bill. White throat and breast, dark gray cap. Gray back. Black wings with white at base of primaries. Tail black with white outer feathers.

Adult Northern Shrike.
Black eyestripe more restricted than Loggerhead; pale broken ring above and below eye. Fine barring on breast. Overall paler gray and larger than Loggerhead.

LOGGERHEAD SHRIKE

Lanius ludovicianus

The raptors of the songbird world, Loggerhead Shrikes, like other shrikes, are known for their adaptive strategy of skewering prey on thorns and barbed wire. Loggerheads are in a long-term decline primarily due to habitat loss.

Open landscapes with good perches and low undergrowth. Hunts insects, reptiles, amphibians, small birds, and mammals. Nests in dense, often thorny, shrubs and low trees.

Uncommon but regular breeder March–September. Look for them at Swanson Lakes WA, Beezley Hills Preserve, North Potholes Reserve, 9 Mile Canyon Road, Virtue Flat, Lawen Marshes, Fort Rock Road, Mann Lake, Borax and Hart Lakes, and Summer Lake WA.

Repeated two-part song, mechanical first part drops, second part whistle rises. Sometimes like Red-winged Blackbird (page 285).

Larger Northern Shrike winters in Loggerhead summer habitat. Lighter gray than Loggerhead, with narrower black mask, white eyeliner above, and white cheek.

Adult.
Pale, rock colored, with fine spotting on back, distinct barring at base of tail. Buffy breast, belly with cinnamon wash. Long, curved bill.

Adult Canyon Wren.
Bolder color and pattern than Rock Wren. White throat, brilliant rufous breast, darker belly. Gray head with fine patterning that extends to rufous back. Bill longer than Rock Wren.

ROCK WREN

Salpinctes obsoletus

What Rock Wrens lack in color and patterning, they make up for in personality. Vibrant, ever-changing songs and with all the right rock moves, they are an endearing bright spot in many canyons.

Dry canyons, rock and talus slopes. Heard more often than seen. Spry and active, commonly seen as a silhouette on boulders and cliff edges. Bounces, bending at the knee. Nests in rock cavities.

Common breeder; rare in winter. Look for them at Sheep Lake, Lake Lenore Caves SP, Columbia NWR, Selah Cliffs Natural Area Preserve, Rhinehart Canyon, John Day Fossil Beds NM, Smith Rock SP, Catlow Valley Road, Hart Mountain, and Fort Rock SP.

Varied, seemingly unrelated series of repeated calls, a fine whistle, then insect-like buzz, cheery rapid staccato.

Canyon Wren with longer bill, shorter tail; dark rusty back, belly, and tail. Call distinct downward spiral.

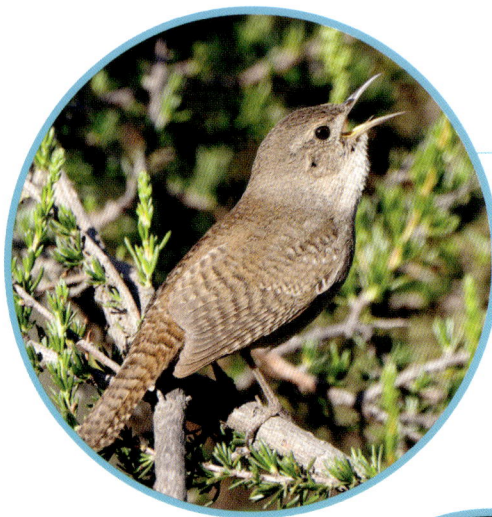

Adult.
Aptly caught with its bill open. Very small, vocal wren. Breast and throat gray. Wings, back, and tail warm brown and barred.

Adult Pacific Wren.
Cinnamon brown all over. Short, spiky tail. Fine barring on belly, wings, and tail. Smaller and with shorter bill than Northern House Wren.

NORTHERN HOUSE WREN

Troglodytes aedon

Northern House Wrens are chattering, fidgety balls of energy, singing happily one minute and scolding the world the next, perhaps protesting the addition of Northern to their name in 2024. They add life and entertainment to many low-elevation habitats.

Open woodlands with shrubby understory, riparian zones, urban landscapes. Energetic to frenetic; often with tail cocked. Forages for insects in low vegetation. Cavity nester, uses almost any cavity, natural or artificial.

Common April–September. Look for them at Iller Creek CA, Mountain View Cemetery, McCartney Creek Preserve, Harder Spring (Kahlotus), Fields Spring and Wallowa Lake SPs, Bird Track Springs, Smith Rock SP, Chukar Park, Page Springs Campground, Hart Mountain, Chandler State Wayside, and Moore Park.

Rapid, buzzy rising chatter, and bubbly falling trills.

Introverted cousins, Pacific Wrens are rarely seen; extravagant song often heard.

LENGTH: 4.75" / WINGSPAN: 6"

Adult.
Brown cap and pale eyebrow distinct; long, slightly downcurved bill. Short, barred tail usually tipped up. Shoulders and rump red-brown.

MARSH WREN

Cistothorus palustris

The frenetic movements of secretive Marsh Wrens may be the result of males simultaneously mating with more than one female. Males build multiple unused nests and, always competing with others, sing endlessly. Both male and female Marsh Wrens will destroy competitors' eggs.

Wetlands, especially cattail and bulrush marshes. Feeds on insects gleaned from foliage and floor of wetland. Often heard but hard to see.

Common summer resident; stays until winter temperatures arrive. Look for them at Cheney Wetlands, Wilson Creek, Quincy WA, Scooteney Reservoir, Lyons Ferry SP, Umatilla NWR, Ladd Marsh WMA, Houston Lakes, Riley Pond, Malheur NWR, Hart Lake, and Klamath WA.

Mostly even, burry, buzzy chatter. Call repeated *tssip*.

Bewick's Wren (page 231) grayer chestnut back and wings with less patterning than Marsh. Bolder white eyebrow, gray belly, white breast.

Adult.
Proportionally long bill, bold white
eyebrow; white throat, gray belly.
Warm brown back, barred tail with
white and black bars on outer edges.

BEWICK'S WREN

Thryomanes bewickii

Once common in the East, Bewick's Wrens retreated West to avoid Northern House Wren competition. Relatively uncommon in eastern Oregon, Bewick's are expanding inland along the Columbia and Snake Rivers.

Shrubby edges, open forest, brush piles. Human habitats; cavity nester. Searches for insects in low vegetation, occasionally on the ground. Cocks tail but also flicks it side to side and fans it, showing black-and-white edges.

Year-round resident; common in Washington, less so in Oregon. Look and listen for them at Myrna Park, Sprague Lake, Sun Lakes SP, Horn Rapids CP, Rock Creek Park, Fort Walla Walla, Enterprise WMA, Cottonwood Canyon SP, Page Springs Campground, and Klamath WA.

Complex trills, whistles, buzzes, not unlike Song Sparrow (page 273). Shorter, more uniform than Pacific Wren (page 226).

Marsh (page 229) and Pacific (page 226) Wrens lack bold, white eyebrow; found in different habitats.

Adult.
Gray-brown head blends smoothly into charcoal-gray body. Long legs pale pink. Short tail often tipped up.

Adult.
In flight, legs tucked up and away. Flat back, round belly.

An adult feeds its chick a small fish.

AMERICAN DIPPER

Cinclus mexicanus

The American Dipper is an iconic mountain stream species. Remaining on open water year-round, even in deep winter cold, dippers are joy.

Clean, fast-flowing mountain streams with structure—boulders, downed logs, overhanging cliffs. Bobs and dips on long legs standing on midstream perches. Dives, swims, and walks underwater foraging for aquatic invertebrates. Nests streamside, usually over water, builds globe-shaped nest of moss on cliffs, tree roots, bridges.

Uncommon year-round resident; often migrates altitudinally, following open water downstream in winter. Look for them at Riverfront Park, Grand Coulee, Kooskooskie, White River Falls SP, Steelhead Falls, Strawberry Lake Trail, Sawyer Park, and Page Springs Campground.

An unlimited series of notes repeated two to four times, each set in the series different—whistles, chatters, buzzes, and mechanical chinks. Call high, buzzy chatter.

There are few things in the world as delightful as dippers.

Breeding adult.
Shiny, sleek, and iridescent
purple and green-black.
Yellow bill; short, square tail.

Nonbreeding adult.
Characteristics include erratic
spotting on belly and flanks; yellow bill and green-black wings
imply molt to breeding plumage.

EUROPEAN STARLING

Sturnus vulgaris

Introduced to Central Park in the 1880s, European Starlings spread to Washington State by the 1950s. With 200 million in North America, starlings are one of the most common birds on the continent. Ironically, the species is declining in some regions of its homeland. Perhaps we can arrange a repatriation.

Human habitats. Large flocks move fluidly in unison. Forages on the ground and hawks swarming insects. Cavity competition from starlings responsible for decline of native cavity-nesting species.

Common year-round. Look for them at Inland Empire Way pond, Columbia NWR, Duffy's Pond, Mt. Hope Cemetery, Enterprise WMA, McKay Creek NWR, Hewitt Park, Arlington, Fossil, Houston Lakes, Rome, Paisley, and Klamath WA.

Varied whistling, popping, electrical, mechanical songs; excels as a mimic.

Blackbirds (pages 279) are similar size but have shorter, more conical bills. Starlings are unique in flight.

Male. Brilliant blue, faint eyeline, white belly and undertail coverts.

Female. Pale eyering. Buffy gray breast and belly. Gray-brown back and wings with faint blue wash. Pale blue tail.

MOUNTAIN BLUEBIRD

Sialia currucoides

Often found at high elevations, these thrushes are more durable than their splendid color indicates. Overwintering and early spring arrival may be a means of beating the competition for nesting cavities.

Open forest and sagebrush with low vegetation, bare ground openings, and suitable nesting cavities. Uses nest boxes and woodpecker holes. Feeds on invertebrates, mostly foraging from ground or low perch.

Year-round, though uncommon in winter in Washington. Look for them at Turnbull NWR, Northrup Canyon, Quilomene WA, Bickleton, Tollgate, Fopiano Reservoir, Unity Lake SP, Idlewild Campground, Crack in the Ground, and Steens, Hart, and Stukel Mountains.

Similar pattern and rhythm as American Robin, less aggressive, softer, more whimsical. Calls often when foraging, low, sweet *freeR*.

Male Western Bluebird indigo blue, with rust breast and flanks. Female Western darker gray with pale rust breastband versus Mountain's soft blue-gray.

Male.
Wide black eyestripe, orange eyebrow.
Deep, black V on breast. Wings strongly
patterned orange and black. Female
overall similar pattern but paler color.

VARIED THRUSH

Ixoreus naevius

Varied Thrushes are known for their summer song and their orange chest with a deep, black V. Habitat loss and fragmentation threaten breeding birds, but winter populations, arriving from the north, appear stable.

Darkest, wettest mature mixed conifer forests and riparian zones; less common in ponderosa pine. Forages on the ground for arthropods in summer; in shrubs and small trees for fruits and berries in fall and winter.

Year-round, though more common in winter. Look and listen for them at Liberty Lake CP, Potholes SP, Leslie Groves Park, Anthony Lake, Smith Rock SP, Page Springs Campground, Summer Lake WA, and Moore Park.

A single, pure whistled note, changing pitch regularly, and repeated ad infinitum. Song sometimes burry or trilled. Also makes soft disturbance and alarm calls.

The comparatively ubiquitous and vociferous American Robin (page 243) lacks the breast V.

Adult.
Spotting distinct on breast, muted on flanks. Rufous color becoming more pronounced from outer wing edges to outer tail feathers. Thin but complete eyering.

Adult Swainson's Thrush.
Muted gray-brown bird with heavily spotted breast, white belly. Buffy eyering appears attached to bill.

HERMIT THRUSH

Catharus guttatus

A widespread but rarely seen bird, Hermit Thrushes have an affinity for dry open forest at higher elevations than most thrushes. Wintering birds stay in North America and segregate by sex, males staying somewhat north of females.

Conifers, mixed deciduous forest with open understory. Feeds on invertebrates, pausing to survey ground between hops. Nests in low vegetation near ground with good surrounding cover.

Common year-round; less so in winter. Look and listen for them at Mountain View Cemetery, Sun Lakes SP, Getty's Cove, Fields Spring and Emigrant Springs SPs, Bear Hollow CP, Crooked River Canyon, Idlewild Campground, Frenchglen, Summer Lake WA, and Putnam's Point.

Long, clear opening note, flutelike, then two to three variable, swirling notes, fading out.

Swainson's Thrush with unique buffy eyering and lores; eyering white in other thrushes. Veery overall brick red; weak breast spots, white belly.

Male.
Bright red breast, black head, striped throat, partial white eyering. Back dark brown-black, black tail. Tips of outer tail feathers white.

Female.
Overall paler than male. Both sexes commonly stretch upright, walk, run, and hop on long legs.

Adult Townsend's Solitaire.
Complete white eyering. Warm gray body and back. Wings with buff-and-black pattern when folded, buffy stripe length of outstretched wing. Outer tail feathers white.

AMERICAN ROBIN

Turdus migratorius

The best-known bird in North America, American Robins sing cheerily across urban and rural landscapes. Highly adaptable to habitats and food sources, robins feed on invertebrates in urban lawns and fall fruits in mountainous terrain.

Early successional and thinned forest. Urbanization increased mixed habitat, which best suits robins. Walks, runs, and hops on the ground; direct flight with short glides between strong wingbeats.

Common year-round resident. Look for them at Riverside and Summer Falls SPs, Columbia NWR, Horn Rapids CP, McNary NWR, Minam State RA, Bird Track Springs, Ochoco Lake CP, Fort Rock Road, Malheur NWR, Fields Oasis, and Hagelstein Park.

High, loud whinny in flight and from treetops. Consistent, repetitive *cheerio cheeriup*. Common call notes include emphatic squeak and *chup chup*.

Smaller Townsend's Solitaire all gray with complete white eyering. Varied Thrush (page 239) smaller and infinitely more introverted.

Adult.
Tawny red crest often appears slicked back; black mask finely edged in white, faint black chin. Buffy brown breast edging into pale yellow belly. White or buff undertail. Tip of tail brilliant yellow.

Adult Bohemian Waxwing.
Cinnamon-colored forehead, tawny crest, black chin. Cinnamon to warm gray back and breast, paler on belly. Rust-colored undertail coverts versus white or buff on Cedar. White wingbars and yellow primary edging distinct.

CEDAR WAXWING

Bombycilla cedrorum

The masked bandits of the bird world, Cedar Waxwings can strip a fruit tree or berry bush in no time flat. An effective disperser of seeds, this species roams all but Arctic North America.

Outside of breeding, forms nomadic flocks commonly found feeding in open woodlands, old fields. Nesting occurs late, timed with ripening late-summer fruit.

Common summer resident. Flocks move incessantly in pursuit of ripe or remaining fruit. Look and listen for them at Liberty Lake CP, Reardan Ponds, Sun Lakes SP, W. E. Johnson Park, Bennington Lake, Maupin City Park, Wallowa Lake and Bates SPs, Malheur NWR, Summer Lake WA, and Moore Park.

High-pitched buzzy, insect-like sound. Noisy but pleasant-sounding flocks easy to track.

Bohemian Waxwings, found irregularly in winter, lack yellow belly; wingtips bright yellow and white, compared to red of Cedar Waxwing.

Adult.
Black bill, pale eyering, and dark eyeline that circles around to define cheek. Strongly striped breast and flanks. Buff undertail. White wingbars.

SAGE THRASHER

Oreoscoptes montanus

A bird that lives exclusively among sagebrush, Sage Thrashers go fly-about during migration, wandering extensively. They will abandon rangeland that is converted to agriculture and urban development or is invaded by introduced grasses.

Sagebrush. Forages on ground for insects. Often runs rather than taking flight. Males sing from visible sagebrush perches. Nests in or under sagebrush.

Fairly common mid-March to September/early October. Look for them at Davenport, Baird Springs Road (Ephrata), Quilomene WA, Rattlesnake Mountain, Virtue Flat, Poison Creek Reservoir, Lawen Marshes, Fields Oasis, Rock Creek Reservoir, Fort Rock SP, and Christmas Valley.

Clear warbling whistles and burry rolling trills; extensive, varied, and unpredictable. The sound of sage steppe in spring.

The smallest and only thrasher commonly seen in this region.

Male.
Slate-gray back, red throat, rusty red breast and belly; black crown and eyeline; white eyebrow. Female with white throat and paler belly and flanks.

Adult White-breasted Nuthatch.
Black crown, eye surrounded by white, no eyestripe. Distinguished from Red-breasted by larger size, all white throat and breast, pale wingbar.

Adult Pygmy Nuthatch.
Gray-brown cap, dark eyeline, white cheeks and throat, pale buff-rust breast with gray flanks. Smaller than Red-breasted, lacks white above eyeline, overall paler coloration.

RED-BREASTED NUTHATCH

Sitta canadensis

Vibrant and feisty, Red-breasted Nuthatches are the most widespread nuthatch and are the sound of winter in conifer forests across North America. They restrict their nesting cavity entrance by applying tree resin to the opening, sometimes using a bit of bark as a tool.

Coniferous forests, especially spruce and fir, from tree line to suburban gardens. Climbs down tree trunk head-first probing for insects; caches seeds. Migrates from the north and from elevation for winter where it often forages with mixed-species flocks.

Common year-round. Look for them at Iller Creek CA, Mountain View Cemetery, Getty's Cove, Washington State University Arboretum, Chiawana Park, Woodward Campground, Smith Rock SP, Walton Lake, Starr Campground, Malheur NWR, Goose Lake State RA, and Moore Park.

Very vocal and insistent. Nasal repeated *whenk*.

Larger White-breasted Nuthatch with white throat, breast, and face; white surrounds eye. Smaller Pygmy Nuthatch with brown head and charcoal-smudged eyeline.

Adult.
Mottled brown-and-black back, buffy wingbars sometimes visible. White throat and breast. Tail frayed looking, used to brace against tree. Long, downcurved bill.

BROWN CREEPER

Certhia americana

Inconspicuous against tree trunks, small spiraling movement is the Brown Creeper's only giveaway. Spending its life entirely on trees, creepers build hammock nests behind loose bark on standing snags.

Mixed woodlands. Breeds in mature and old-growth forests with standing snags. Spirals tree trunk from base up; gleans insect larvae and eggs from bark furrows. Drops like a falling leaf from upper trunk to base of next tree.

Common year-round. Wintering birds favor lowlands. Look for them at Liberty Lake CP, Mountain View Cemetery, Crescent Bar, Lyons Ferry SP, Biscuit Ridge Road, Smith Rock SP, Barnhouse and Page Springs Campgrounds, Hart Mountain, and Moore Park.

High-pitched song. Two high notes, drop, return: *Tsi tsi zu zu zu tsi.*

Red-breasted Nuthatch (page 249) is of similar size and shape, but coloration and movement dissimilar. Nuthatches work down trees; creepers work up.

Male.
Red head, back, and breast. Red head does not extend to nape. Heavy conical bill. Brown streaks on flanks; long tail.

Female.
Brown overall, streaked breast and back. Conical bill. Almost square tail.

Male Cassin's Finch.
Red crest. Less extensive red on throat and breast than House. No streaking on breast or flanks. Cassin's female with whiter face, more pronounced crest, and sharper, more defined streaks on breast than House female. Cassin's male and female with larger, pointier bill, and notched tail.

Male Purple Finch.
Red wash over head, breast, and back. Light eyebrow. Faint striping smudged across belly. Female Purple browner with more distinct markings than House. Purple with notched tail.

HOUSE FINCH

Haemorhous mexicanus

Native to the Southwest, House Finches introduced to the East in the 1950s eventually integrated with western populations expanding north and east. House Finches now span the continent.

Lowland brushy fields, open forest and edges, human habitats. Postbreeding flocks move to drier sites. Forages for seeds on the ground, in shrubs and trees. Readily visits bird feeders.

Common and widespread year-round. Look for them at Morrow Park, Harrington Cemetery, Dry Falls, Martha Lake, Chief Timothy Park, Cold Springs NWR, Rhinehart Canyon, Crooked River and Bully Creek Campgrounds, Jordan Valley, and Plush Community Park.

Long series of chip, chirp, *tzzeee* notes, often ending with a buzzy *zzzzzzzzzt*.

Finches best distinguished by habitat. Cassin's prefers dry mountain forest, ponderosa pine and Douglas fir. Purple Finches prefer mixed deciduous and riparian forest; both less associated with humans but use feeders during local migrations.

LENGTH: 6" / WINGSPAN: 10"

Male.
Red-brown cheek. Matte red head, breast, and belly; reddish brown wings and back.

Female.
Olive-yellow-green brightest on back. Pale gray throat. Dark wings, notched tail.

Juvenile.
Brown overall, often streaked. Crossed bill develops after fledging.

RED CROSSBILL

Loxia curvirostra

A complex species spanning the northern latitudes, Red Crossbill subspecies are primarily divided by call type. Each type is highly adapted to its preferred conifer species, with bill length and cross depth dependent on cone structure.

Mature conifer forests. Population variable and mobile; flocks follow cone crop density. Nesting may occur throughout the year and is timed with seed availability. Young develop crossed bills within a month of fledging.

Common but unreliable in any given location. Look for them at Myrna Park, Steptoe Butte SP, Lewis Peak, Hilgard Junction SP, Bear Hollow CP, Delintment Lake, Malheur NWR, Cabin Lake, and Moore Park.

Simple *tchip tchip* series of two to twelve; often given in flight. Song not commonly heard.

White-winged Crossbill rare and often not seen for years at a time. Other finches smaller, lack crossed bills.

Breeding male.
Crisp colors, wingbars, and orange bill. Undertail coverts white.

Nonbreeding male.
Retains black-and-white wings but trades yellow body feathers and black cap for tan with yellow wash.

Female with chicks.
Pale grayish yellow body, lacks black forehead of male. Pale wingbars.

Male Lesser Goldfinch.
Black cap goes through eye. Yellow-green back; wings black, more yellow-green than American. Undertail coverts yellow.

Male Pine Siskin.
Head and back streaked brown, breast white with sturdy brown streaks. Faint brown arc from eye to shoulder. Yellow wingbar and edging, primaries with yellow wash, yellow at upper base of tail. Female with muted streaking. Streaking distinct compared with goldfinches.

AMERICAN GOLDFINCH

Spinus tristis

Familiar visitors to thistle feeders, American Goldfinches are acrobatic foragers found in small summer foraging groups and large winter flocks. Whiny call notes and undulating flight make birds visible despite drab winter plumage.

Lowlands, forages in open landscapes, nests in trees. Initiates nesting late to time hatching with thistle seed set. Feeds almost exclusively on seeds.

Common year-round. Look for them at Morrow Park, Wilson Creek, Harder Spring (Kahlotus), Coppei Creek, Rhinehart Canyon, Hatfield Lake, Chukar Park, Catlow Valley Road, and Klamath WA.

Series of twittering tweets, slurred at the end into a burry buzz. Often calls in flight *phew twee twee twee*, and a chattering barrage of notes.

Pine Siskin similar to female goldfinch, but uniformly brown striped; male with yellow wingbars. Lesser Goldfinch male more olive, dark armpits, white wing patches, white outer tail; female more uniform coloring, lacks defined yellow shoulder.

Breeding adult.
Rufous cap edged with white, black eyestripe. Buffy gray breast, notched tail. Rufous-and-black wings with white wingbars. In nonbreeding adults, cap paler rufous, edged with tan; black eyeline still distinct.

Adult Brewer's Sparrow.
A fairly standard sparrow. Complete white eyering. Bill smaller than Chipping Sparrow's, more buffy tan back, and wingbars discreet to invisible.

CHIPPING SPARROW

Spizella passerina

Chipping Sparrows are stylish with rufous caps, black eyelines, and distinct rust-and-black striped backs and wings. Among the many similar sparrows, it stands out. Its song is also simple and easy to identify. Finally, a sparrow not incognito.

Dry conifer, especially ponderosa pine, woodland and edges. Forages on ground for grass seeds; includes invertebrates when nesting. Flocks out of breeding season. Sings persistently from visible perch.

Common summer resident April–October. Look for them at Philleo Lake, Steptoe Butte and Potholes SPs, Wanapum RA, Bennington Lake, Cold Springs NWR, Rhinehart Canyon, Walton Lake, Idlewild Campground, Leslie Gulch, Frenchglen, Hart Mountain, and Moore Park.

Single uniform trill, mechanical, sometimes lengthy. Somewhat junco-like, less sweet and bell-like.

Brewer's Sparrow lacks Chipping's chestnut cap and prefers sagebrush with scattered juniper.

Adult.
Rufous-and-white striped head, black eyeline, rufous cheek. Black mustache, white breast with notable black center spot. Back buffy gray, wings shades of brown. Undertail white, outer tail feathers white and evident.

**Breeding male
House Sparrow.**
Pale gray belly, black bib. Gray cap and rufous eyestripe. Heavy bill. Female with pale, unmarked gray-brown throat and breast, striped back, faint wingbar. Non-breeding male with white wingbar, less distinct black bib.

LARK SPARROW

Chondestes grammacus

Extremely territorial during breeding season, male Lark Sparrows spar with other males that invade their space, and court the females that cross the line. After hatching, they are all friends again and return to flocking.

Open grasslands, sage steppe with scattered trees, shrubs, bare ground. Walks preferentially; flight is direct, low. Ground forager for insects and seeds, heavy on insects when nesting. Nests on or near ground.

Locally common breeder late April–September. Look for them at Turnbull NWR, Beezley Hills Preserve, Horn Rapids CP, 9 Mile Canyon Road, Thief Valley Reservoir, John Day Fossil Beds NM, Crooked River Wetlands Complex, Leslie Gulch, Catlow Valley Road, and Summer Lake WA.

Disjointed but continuous series of trills, buzzes, whistles. Males often sing from treetops.

House Sparrow male with black throat, gray cap and cheek, chestnut back, short tail.

Male.
Dark hood and throat, pink bill, upper back rusty, flanks brick-colored. Outer tail feathers in male and female white. Slate-colored male uniformly gray, lacks hood and coloring.

Female.
Gray hood and throat paler than male, pink bill, reddish wash in brown flanks and back, white breast. Slate-colored female grayer, darker overall.

Immature.
Mottled gray head, rusty back. Wings gray and rufous. Belly buffy, streaky with rufous wash.

DARK-EYED JUNCO

Junco hyemalis

The bell-like song of Dark-eyed Juncos is a bright spot during Northwest winters. Two subspecies are found in eastern Washington and Oregon: year-round resident Oregon Juncos and uncommon winter residents Slate-colored Juncos.

Nests and forages on ground in shrubby coniferous forest. Feeds on seeds and invertebrates. Winters in open woodlands, forest edges; seen regularly in small flocks and at bird feeders. Males begin singing from treetops in midwinter.

Common throughout, but more often seen in winter. Look for them at Iller Creek CA, Mountain View Cemetery, Getty's Cove, Palouse Falls SP, Chief Timothy Park, Wallowa Lake SP, Morgan Lake, Ochoco Divide Campground, Fields Oasis, and Hagelstein Park.

Song rapid, musical series much like Chipping Sparrow, sweeter and less mechanical.

Larger size, dark back, black bill, and red eye differentiate Spotted Towhee (page 275). Juvenile juncos may be confused with other sparrows.

Adult.
Black-and-white striped head, last black stripe extending from back of eye; gray cheek, throat, and neck; orange bill. Streaked back and wings shades of brown, rufous, and gray. Wingtips often held below body and tail.

Juvenile (first winter).
Yellow bill unlike gray bill in juvenile Golden-crowned Sparrow. Rufous head stripes.

Breeding adult Golden-crowned Sparrow.
Bicolored bill, yellow crown, black through eye. No white on head or face; chestnut flanks.

WHITE-CROWNED SPARROW

Zonotrichia leucophrys

This dapper sparrow is familiar throughout the Pacific Northwest and most of the continent. Despite benefiting from brushy habitat created by forest clearing, White-crowned Sparrow populations show a significant long-term decline in many western habitats.

Brushy landscapes, forest edges; winters in lowlands. Rarely found away from adequate cover; flits to safety rapidly and regularly. Ground forager for insects, seeds, and fruits.

Common summer resident; locally common in winter. Look for them at Liberty Lake CP, Granite Lake, Dry Falls, Potholes SP, Washtucna, Itani Park, McNary NWR, Cottonwood Canyon SP, Fossil, North Powder Pond, Powell Butte, Malheur NWR, Steens Mountain, Silver Lake, and Putnam's Point.

Familiar song is a pure, sweet whistle followed by jumbled notes and a burry trill.

Yellow crown bordered by black stripes and dark bill separates Golden-crowned Sparrow.

LENGTH: 7" / WINGSPAN: 9.5"

Adult.
Broad gray eyestripe; head peaked at back; fine streaking on breast, back, and flanks. Pale buffy mustache stripe.

LINCOLN'S SPARROW

Melospiza lincolnii

The elusive Lincoln's Sparrow is easily overlooked. A common winter resident, birds may have moved from higher elevation breeding sites or south from the boreal forests of Alaska and Canada.

Shrubby willow thickets, dense riparian vegetation at elevation. Secretive. Sings from low perch; moves away from nest through tunnels in underbrush. Individuals sometimes flock with other sparrows in winter. Feeds on seeds and invertebrates.

Common migrant; summer breeder at elevation. Look for them at Turnbull NWR, Sun Lakes and Potholes SPs, Bateman Island, Rooks Park, Ladd Marsh WMA, Hatfield Lake, Malheur NWR, Fields Oasis, Summer Lake WA, and Lake Ewauna Nature Trail.

Unhurried, liquid song; rising notes, a trill, descending finish. Wren-like.

Song Sparrow (page 273) larger, longer-tailed, darker.

Adult.
Pale gray-brown overall, fine streaking on back and wings. Grayish white breast with central black spot.

Adult.
Complete white eyering. Pale spots between eyes and bill (lores). Fine streaking on throat. Outer tail edges white.

SAGEBRUSH SPARROW

Artemisiospiza nevadensis

Although often well hidden in tall shrubs, male Sagebrush Sparrows sing from obvious perches. Sagebrush Sparrows typically raise two broods. In late summer, adults and fledglings from the second clutch join flocks of early summer juveniles.

Mature sagebrush in the Columbia Plateau and southeast Oregon. Ground forager for invertebrates in summer, seeds in winter. Runs between shrubs, chin down, tail up; commonly runs when startled. Nests near or on ground. Holds and defends large territory.

Uncommon and local summer resident March–August. Look for them at Saddle Mountain NWR, Rattlesnake Mountain, Fort Rock Road, Chickahominy Reservoir, Malheur NWR, Borax Lake, Hart Mountain, and Summer Lake WA.

A buzzy introduction to a fluty and variable song, both given twice before pausing and repeating.

Gray head, tan back, and central black breast spot unique.

LENGTH: 6" / WINGSPAN: 8.25"

Adult.
Back finely patterned. White throat; streaked breast often with center V, white belly. Head with pale center stripe; buffy mustache, dark eyeline. Feathers between bill and eye (lores) usually yellow.

Adult Vesper Sparrow.
Facial markings similar to and paler than Savannah. Streaked throat and weak center spot. White outer tail feathers best dividing characteristic.

SAVANNAH SPARROW

Passerculus sandwichensis

The Savannah Sparrow song is the sound of summer grasslands. Found breeding from coast to coast and north to the Arctic Ocean, Savannah Sparrows inhabit most open landscapes.

Grasslands, overgrown pastures, weedy wastelands. Sings often and loudly from visible perch. Ground nester; scurries away from nest like a mouse through grasses. Feeds on insects and invertebrates.

Common breeder; rare in winter. Look and listen for them at Saltese Flats, Crab Creek drainage, Columbia and McNary NWRs, Zumwalt Prairie, Smith Rock SP, Silvies Valley, Steens and Hart Mountains, Paisley, and Wood River Wetland.

Ts ts tstup tup tup TSeeeee tsree, relatively even, high-pitched series of chips and trills; oft repeated.

Vesper Sparrow with fine white eyering, white outer tail feathers, buff belly. Song Sparrow (page 273) larger, darker, un-notched tail.

Adult.
Brown-and-white striped throat, white belly. Relatively long, un-notched tail.

Adult.
Brown crown with gray central stripe, dark eyestripe from back of eye. Brown-and-gray striped breast forming neat center V more than a breast spot.

SONG SPARROW

Melospiza melodia

Widely distributed across the continent, Song Sparrows have a remarkable repertoire of songs. Living up to their name, both males and females sing year-round.

Brushy, open woodland, riparian zones, wetlands. Sings incessantly. Nests near or on the ground. Forages on or near the ground, often at water's edge with feet in the water; eats seeds, fruit, invertebrates.

Common year-round resident. Look and listen for them at Dishman Hills NA, Reardan Ponds, Gloyd Seeps Wetland, Wawawai CP, Coppei Creek, McNary NWR, DeMoss Springs Memorial Park, Poison Creek Reservoir, Catlow Valley Road, Riley Pond, Putnam's Point.

A melodious series of introductory chips, a long trill, final descending notes.

Fox Sparrow breast more spotted than streaked; lacks head patterning. Savannah Sparrow (page 271) with yellow lores and notched tail.

Male.
Black head and throat, red eye. Back with white spots; long black tail, outer tail feather tips white.

Female.
Similar pattern as male, including white breast and rust-colored flanks; rich brown instead of black. Pale eye.

Adult Green-tailed Towhee.
Rufous cap, white throat streaks. Pale gray breast, buff belly. Back gray-green; wings and tail bright olive-green.

SPOTTED TOWHEE

Pipilo maculatus

A cheerful reminder to look closely at scrubby habitat, Spotted Towhees are often heard in deep thickets unfit for humans. Their red eyes and white-spotted coat are snappy and sophisticated among the brambles.

Shrubby habitat, mid- to low elevations. Forest edges, brushy canyons, dense thickets. Secretive and solitary, but often sings and calls. Forages in the leaf litter with a double-legged scratch; feeds on invertebrates, seeds, and fruit.

Common summer resident; regular in winter. Look and listen for them at Turnbull NWR, Douglas Creek, Rose Creek Nature Preserve, Hat Rock SP, Dyer State Wayside, Theimer Canyon, Leslie Gulch, Chandler State Wayside, and Wood River Wetland.

Complex series of high squeaks and trills, *chechecheT-Zeeee*. Varied and variable.

Smaller Green-tailed Towhee found in similar habitats, but rufous cap, yellow-green back distinct. Pale flanks, pink bill, white outer tail feathers differentiate Dark-eyed Junco (page 263).

Adult.
Bright yellow breast, gray head becoming more olive down back. Long tail.

Adult.
White eyering and spectacles. Stout bill. White belly and undertail coverts.

YELLOW-BREASTED CHAT

Icteria virens

Although bright yellow birds stand out, Yellow-breasted Chats perfected the disappearing act. In an unexpected avian twist, males and females take nighttime journeys beyond breeding territories to mingle with others' mates.

Dense, brushy habitat with open canopy, usually near water. Secretive. Females stay near the ground always; males visible when singing in breeding season. Nests and forages near ground; feeds on invertebrates, some fruits.

Locally common May–September. Look for them at Dishman Hills NA, Frenchman Coulee, Columbia NWR, Alpowa Creek, McNary NWR, Cottonwood Canyon SP, Chukar Park, Leslie Gulch, Fields Oasis, Summer Lake WA, and Putnam's Point.

Extensive repertoire of whistles, stutters, trills evenly spaced between call type. Chatters, deeper and slower than orioles and wrens.

Brightly colored birds of a different feather, Bullock's Oriole and Western Tanager (pages 283 and 303) easily separated by habits and habitats.

Male.
Brilliant yellow head and throat, black eye, and strong black bill. All-black body and tail. Black wings with white primary coverts, not always visible when perched, but obvious in flight.

Female.
Head mottled orange-brown, bright yellow bib. Dark brown body, wings, and tail.

YELLOW-HEADED BLACKBIRD

Xanthocephalus xanthocephalus

The bullies of the marsh, Yellow-headed Blackbirds arrive late to the breeding grounds and muscle Red-winged Blackbirds out of prime nesting locations. Loosely colonial, Yellow-headed males manage a harem of one to six females that nest within the male's territory. Females protect their nest's immediate surroundings but ignore male territorial boundaries.

Desert wetlands, mountain and aspen wet meadows. Nests in cattails and bulrushes over deep water. Feeds on aquatic invertebrates during breeding. Loud and vocal, not easily missed.

Common summer resident March–September, sometimes overwinters. Look for them at Philleo Lake, Dry Falls, Savage Pond, Amon Creek, Quesna CP, Fopiano and Poison Creek Reservoirs, Catlow Valley Road, Adel Ponds, Christmas Valley, and Klamath WA.

Like Red-winged Blackbird but less bubbly. *Ki ki ki ki kiiiiir.*

Male's bold yellow head, female's pale yellow head and brown body unique.

LENGTH: 9.5" / WINGSPAN: 15"

Breeding adult.
Prominent bill. Yellow
lores, black eyestripe
extending back from eye.
Uniform fine patterning
on back, wings, and tail.

Breeding adult.
Brilliant yellow throat, breast,
and belly; flanks white, dark
spotted. Deep black V on chest.
Nonbreeding birds paler overall.

WESTERN MEADOWLARK

Sturnella neglecta

One of the most ubiquitous birds of open country, Western Meadowlarks are the soundtrack of grasslands and sagebrush steppe alike. Vibrant, visible, and vocal, meadowlarks never fail to delight.

Grasslands, sage steppe, crop edges, roadsides. Feeds on the ground. Foods shift seasonally, insects through breeding, grain and seeds in fall and winter. Male often sings from visible perch. In flight, rapid wingbeats interspersed with glides.

Common summer resident, uncommon local winterer. Look for them at Saltese Flats, Moses Coulee, Priest Rapids Dam, Anatone Flats, Zumwalt Prairie, Spring Creek and Trout Creek Campgrounds, Chickahominy Reservoir, Burns Junction, Hart and Silver Lakes, and Klamath WA.

Sweet whistled warble opening with clear whistled notes, ending with bubbly gurgle. In-flight call single clear whistle. Call note *chik*.

Deep black V across bold yellow breast distinct. White outer tail feathers evident in flight.

Male.
Black cap, throat, and eyeline. Fine, sharp bill. Eyebrow and cheek golden orange. Breast orange fading to yellow belly, undertail coverts. Dark back. Dark wings with white epaulets (secondaries) and white-streaked primaries.

Female.
Olive and yellow-orange head, cheeks, and throat. Breast and belly buffy yellow, brightening yellow undertail coverts. Back gray-brown with similar but fainter wing pattern as male.

BULLOCK'S ORIOLE

Icterus bullockii

A brilliant orange bird with a beautiful song, gossipy chatter, and fine weaving skills, Bullock's Oriole is always welcome in cottonwood galleries along waterways throughout the dry side.

Mature riparian forest, isolated large trees like those around old homesteads. Mostly gleans insects in canopy, also eats fruit and nectar. Carefully woven dangling nest, unique and distinct.

Common summer resident May–August. Look for them at Saltese Flats, Steamboat Rock SP, Ancient Lakes, Lewis & Clark Trail SP, Rhinehart Canyon, Maupin City and Chukar Parks, Rome, Malheur NWR, Goose Lake State RA, Silver Lake, and Hagelstein Park.

Series of husky chatter and clear whistles with two or three introductory notes, a spiked *wee*, and variable whistle.

Smaller Yellow-breasted Chat (page 277) yellow and olive, lacks white wing patches. Black-headed Grosbeak (page 305) male with all-black head, female with white eyebrow and mustache.

Breeding male.
Brilliant orange-red wing patch (lesser coverts) edged with pale yellow-orange. Remainder of wing and bird all black.

Female.
Brown overall with dense, even streaking. Fine, sharp bill. Pale eyestripe.

Male Tricolored Blackbird.
Nearly identical to Red-winged. Wing patches deep blood red edged at bottom with buffy white.

RED-WINGED BLACKBIRD

Agelaius phoeniceus

Red-winged Blackbirds are complicated. Males aggressively defend territories holding numerous females, and females regularly find secondary partners, forming an elaborate social structure. Still one of the most abundant North American birds, the population has declined by 36 percent since the 1960s.

Wetlands, lake edges, ditches, almost any waterbody. Feeds primarily on the ground. Forms enormous flocks out of breeding season. Will stay on territories year-round if weather and foraging conditions permit.

Common year-round resident. Look for them at Saltese Flats, Summer Falls SP, Sentinel Bluffs, Harder Spring (Kahlotus), Chief Timothy Park, Ladd Marsh WMA, White River Falls SP, Poison Creek and Antelope Reservoirs, Lake Abert, and Stevenson Park.

Complex bubbling, gurgling, and chatter. *EerrEerr eerrRRREE.*

Tricolored Blackbird male wing patches dark red and white versus Red-winged's orange-red and yellow; female more gray, with whitish throat. Uncommon, local throughout region.

LENGTH: 8.75" / WINGSPAN: 13"

Adult male.
Dark brown head; black iridescent body. Black conical bill.

Female.
Pale throat, pale eyebrow, heavy bill. Fine streaking on breast, back uniformly brown and finely patterned.

Immature male.
Overall pale tan, dark wings, iridescence barely visible.

BROWN-HEADED COWBIRD

Molothrus ater

Once following bison herds across the Great Plains, Brown-headed Cowbirds didn't linger to raise chicks. Instead, they laid eggs in other species' nests and moved on. Livestock and agriculture facilitated range expansion to the detriment of unsuspecting host birds. First recorded breeding in Washington State in the 1950s, cowbirds are now ubiquitous.

Grasslands, open woodlands. Hunts insects on ground, often near livestock. A brood parasite, female lays as many as 40 eggs per year. Flocks with other blackbirds in winter.

Common breeder; uncommon year-round resident. Look for them at Granite and Jameson Lakes, Wanapum RA, Pampa Pond, Two Rivers and Maupin City Parks, Clyde Holliday State RA, Lawen Marshes, Fort Rock SP, Page Springs Campground, and Paisley.

Alternately bubbling and high-pitched *glupUP tse*; female chatters.

Brewer's Blackbird (page 289) male lacks brown head; female with larger bill, overall brighter coloration.

Male.
Shiny black at first glance. Head with deep purple sheen; body glossy green-black. Light iris.

Female.
Fine, black bill. Uniformly brown overall with little patterning and slightest sheen.

BREWER'S BLACKBIRD

Euphagus cyanocephalus

Brewer's Blackbirds readily expanded with human development. Following agriculture, roads, and building, the range of these once-western birds now extends across the Southeast and north into Canada.

Open landscape, agriculture, human-altered habitat. Forages primarily on ground for insects, seeds, and grains; walks rather than hops. Colonial nester; colony location tied directly to foraging opportunity. Individual nest site based on availability of forage and perches.

Common breeder; local in winter. Look for them at Liberty Lake CP, Jameson Lake, County Line Ponds, Anatone Flats, McNary and Umatilla NWRs, Maupin City Park, Rimrock Springs WMA, Big Summit Prairie, Rock Creek Reservoir, Christmas Valley, and Upper Klamath Lake.

CchHUP chHup tsEE; calls high-pitched, can be bubbly or mechanical.

Red-winged Blackbird (page 285) female with distinct eyeline, striped breast. Brown-headed Cowbird (page 287) male head lacks iridescence; female uniformly brown with conical bill.

Adult.
Mostly yellow breast and belly with faint streaks. Uniformly colored.

Adult.
Olive back, dark wing edges, olive-gray tail. Incomplete eyering, subtle light eyebrow, and fine eyeline; long, sharply pointed bill.

Adult Nashville Warbler.
Complete white eyering. Head and back gray. Throat, breast, and belly uniformly yellow. Wings olive-yellow. Breeding male with few rusty spots on crown.

ORANGE-CROWNED WARBLER

Leiothlypis celata

Widespread Orange-crowned Warblers are one of few warblers more common in the West than the East. Highly variable songs are distinct enough to distinguish individual males.

Shrubby lowlands; riparian willows, alders, and maples; mixed forest with dense understory. Nests on or near ground and gleans insects from vegetation. Also feeds from sapsucker holes and can hover to pick prey from vegetation.

Fairly common breeder April–October. Look for them at Turnbull NWR, McCosh Park, Horn Rapids CP, Fields Spring SP, Zumwalt Prairie, Shelton Wayside CP, Smith Rock SP, Theimer Canyon, Steens Mountain, Summer Lake WA, and Eagle Ridge/Shoalwater Bay.

Song nondescript warble, trilled but tune relatively flat, ending with several lower notes. Call abrupt, rising *jit*.

Nashville Warbler with gray head, yellow throat and breast, olive-green wings and back; sharp, white eyering.

Immature male.
Black eye band with yellow spot below eye. Fine black bill. Black throat, yellow breast and belly, black-streaked flanks. Adult male with deep black throat and crown, pronounced black streaks on flanks.

Adult female.
Face and head pattern like male but olive-green. Breast and face yellow. Male and female with gray wings, white wingbars.

TOWNSEND'S WARBLER

Setophaga townsendi

A habitat generalist in migration, Townsend's Warblers nest in conifer forests from Oregon to Alaska. Summer and breeding ranges are relatively constricted compared to the expanse of the West used in migration. Birds winter along the Pacific Coast from Vancouver to Baja and inland from central Mexico to Central America.

Mature conifer forests; prefers fir. Territorial. Forages and nests high in dense canopy. Feeds on insects, especially spruce budworm.

Common summer resident late April–August, migrants into mid-October. Look for them at Mica Peak Conservation Area, Mountain View Cemetery, Oasis Park (Ephrata), Bennington Lake, Emigrant Springs and Smith Rock SPs, Strawberry Lake Trail, Malheur NWR, Fields Oasis, and Moore Park.

High, sweet whistles followed by rising buzzy, slurred notes.

Even among the slew of black-and-yellow warblers, Townsend's stands out.

Male.
Black mask with white forehead, greenish yellow head. Bright yellow throat, olive-gray or yellow belly. Olive-green back.

Female.
Pale yellow-brown overall. Throat and undertail coverts yellow. Disproportionately long bill.

Female MacGillivray's Warbler.
Gray hood, yellow belly, olive-gray back. Male with slate-gray hood, black lores, and bright white partial eyeliner above and below eyes.

COMMON YELLOWTHROAT

Geothlypis trichas

A reclusive but vociferous bird of dense, wet, shrubby places. Males are conspicuous and easily identified when openly perching to sing. Females are particularly cagey during nesting season and rarely seen.

Low, wet areas of early successional growth and cattail wetlands. Behavior wren-like and secretive; often wags tail and moves furtively through shrubs.

Locally common lowland breeder. Look and listen for them at Saltese Flats, Sun Lakes SP, Getty's Cove, Wawawai CP, Whitman Mission National Historic Site, Umatilla NWR, Crooked River Wetlands Complex, Forest Conservation Area (Prairie City), Fields Oasis, Summer Lake WA, and Putnam's Point.

Three to five series of *witchety witchety witchety*, oft repeated. Some regional variation. Call sharp *cheat*.

Females may be confused with female Yellow (more yellow, page 297) and Orange-crowned (more olive, page 291) Warblers. MacGillivray's Warbler with gray hood (females paler than males).

Male.
Bright yellow throat and breast with rust-colored streaks. Head, back, and wings olive-yellow. Relatively long, black bill.

Female.
Bright yellow head, throat, breast, and belly. Olive wings and back. Thin black bill. Female lacks breast streaks.

Female Wilson's Warbler.
Bright yellow breast and belly, speckled black cap, olive-yellow back and wings. Male with distinct black cap.

YELLOW WARBLER

Setophaga petechia

Feisty little birds with big personalities, Yellow Warblers are among the most widespread and common of all warblers. No less engaging, the bright yellow flash with chestnut streaks is a spring delight.

Brushy wet or disturbed areas; commonly associated with willows, but old fields also readily occupied. Flits rapidly through branches gleaning insects from leaves and bark.

Common summer resident late April–early October. Look and listen for them at Iller Creek CA, Potholes SP, Sentinel Bluffs, Harder Spring (Kahlotus), Jasper Mountain, Plymouth and Maupin City Parks, Mitchell, Juntura, Malheur NWR, Cottonwood Creek (Fields), Paulina Marsh, and Putnam's Point.

Rapid-fire, high, clear song, *sweet sweet sweet little more sweet.* Loud simple chip call.

Orange-crowned Warbler's (page 291) overall green tinge, fine dark eyeline separates from female Yellow. Wilson's Warbler female lacks white wing edges, male sports black cap.

Breeding male Audubon's.
Bright yellow throat, yellow crown, black breastband with yellow edges, white belly and undertail. Yellow rump.

Nonbreeding male Audubon's.
In nonbreeding plumage, scant black breastband. Yellow rump visible in flight year-round.

Female Audubon's.
Gray face and head, partial eyering, yellow throat. Breeding birds with darker streaked breast, yellow flanks. White wingbars, yellow rump.

YELLOW-RUMPED WARBLER

Setophaga coronata

Wildly varied and widely distributed, two Yellow-rumped Warbler subspecies appear on the East Side. Audubon's Warbler, with a yellow throat, are the primary breeders, while Myrtle Warbler, with a white throat, is transitory.

Open coniferous, mixed deciduous forest. Gleans and hawks insects, invertebrates from foliage, bark, and ground.

Audubon's common migrant and breeder; occasional in winter. Myrtle uncommon migrant. Look for them at Saltese Flats, Northrup Canyon, Getty's Cove, Wawawai CP, Woodward Campground, Arlington, Maupin City Park, Hatfield Lake, Idlewild Campground, Hart Mountain, Cabin Lake, and Hagelstein Park.

Song relatively weak beginning and end; clear warbled notes in between. Subspecies calls differ: flat *chip* for Myrtle; brighter, higher *tsip* for Audubon's.

Yellow rump visible in winter plumage when confusion with sparrows is possible. Townsend's Warbler (page 293) has a black throat and yellow breast, the opposite of Yellow-rumped.

LENGTH: 5.5" / WINGSPAN: 9.25"

Male.
Chunky bird with heavy greenish bill. Brilliant yellow forehead and under-tail coverts. Cap, face, and throat black grading into deep yellow breast and belly; back deeper shade. Black wings, white wing coverts, black tail.

Female.
Large bill more olive-green. Gray head and back with yellow defining back of neck and shoulders. Breast and belly buffy tan, white undertail coverts. Black-and-white wings and tail.

Male Pine Grosbeak.
Larger than Evening with smaller head and bill. Red head, body, and back. Gray flanks. Brown wings and tail with pink wash. White wingbars.

Female Pine Grosbeak.
Head yellow-green, gray eye. Gray overall, breast with yellow-green wash. Wingbars distinct.

EVENING GROSBEAK

Coccothraustes vespertinus

Although Evening Grosbeaks range across much of North America, they are irruptive, and predicting their next move is near impossible. Their most reliable address is bird feeders in spring.

Mid- to high-elevation coniferous forest. Flocking, gregarious, and noisy. Nests high in canopy. Feeds on insects, fruits, and seeds. Strips fleshy fruit from seeds with beak before cracking and swallowing the seed.

Fairly common breeder; uncommon in winter. Location throughout the year unpredictable. Look for them at Iller Creek CA, Potholes SP, Kamiak Butte CP, Bennington Lake, Joseph, Malheur NWR, Fields Oasis, Summer Lake WA, and Moore Park.

Almost insect-like buzz. *Brrrrrt.*

Pinkish red Pine Grosbeak males easily distinguished; females differentiated by markedly smaller, hooked bill, and white wingbars on Pine versus white wing patches in Evening.

Breeding adults.
Male (right): Upper back and wings black. Yellow shoulder, white wingbar. Female (left): Overall pale olive, brighter breast and belly; wings with evident pale bars.

Breeding male.
Bright yellow breast, collar, belly, and rump. Scarlet forehead, throat, and cheeks.

WESTERN TANAGER

Piranga ludoviciana

Could there be anything showier than a male Western Tanager? Its brilliant colors move up the food chain from plants that produce the color compound to plant-eating insects to the canopy-gleaning tanager.

Coniferous and mixed forest; appears to use all age stands with a slight preference for mature forest. Feeds on insects high in treetops. Often feeds on fruit, moves in small flocks when migrating.

Common breeder and migrant May–September. Look for them at Turnbull NWR, Ginkgo Petrified Forest SP, Central Ferry HMU, Minam State RA, DeMoss Springs Memorial Park, Smith Rock SP, Theimer Canyon, Pike Creek, Plush Community Park, Cabin Lake, and Wood River Wetland.

Call rapid *purDWeet*. Song reminiscent of American Robin but shorter, less insistent, burrier.

Females larger than other similarly colored warblers and finches. Less common Bullock's Oriole (page 283) female with white wingbars and gray body.

Male.
Thick bill; black head, orange collar and breast, white undertail. Bold black-and-white wings.

Female.
White eyebrow and crown stripe bordered with brown; white mustache stripe; pale orange breast fading to tan belly; white wingbars. Juveniles notably have similar facial pattern.

BLACK-HEADED GROSBEAK

Pheucticus melanocephalus

Spring migration brings adult male Black-headed Grosbeaks first; adult females follow. Finally, juvenile males arrive in varying stages of adult male plumage. This distinct schedule seems to reduce older male aggression toward juveniles competing for breeding rights.

Elsewhere a habitat generalist, Washington and Oregon birds prefer deciduous riparian forest with brushy understory. Uses urban habitat with suitable cover and food sources. Gleans vegetation for insects, spiders, seeds, and fruit.

Common breeder May to August. Look and listen for them at Turnbull and Columbia NWRs, Coppei Creek, McNary NWR, Crooked River Wetlands Complex, Clyde Holliday State RA, Bullard Canyon, Fort Rock SP, and Moore Park.

More discrete than run-on American Robin. Distinct trills interspersed in longer song, pauses between repetitions.

Less common Bullock's Oriole (page 283) has orange face, yellow-orange eyebrow, black eyeline and throat, pointed bill, more white on wings.

LENGTH: 8.25" / WINGSPAN: 12.5"

Male.
Lapis-blue head, back, and rump; wings and tail darker. Black eye and bill. Neck rust-colored blending into bright white breast and belly. Strong white wingbars.

Female.
Rusty-buff head and body, no patterning. Wings and tail dark brown, rusty-buff wingbars.

LAZULI BUNTING

Passerina amoena

Lazuli Bunting males have a unique means of acquiring their song—they essentially learn the neighborhood dialect. Using elements of songs from older males, they piece together a unique arrangement. Once decided, they don't vary from their composition.

Dry, brushy slopes, draws, riparian areas, recent burns. Feeds on insects, fruits, seeds, and grain. Forages on the ground, on grasses, and in tree canopies. Gleans insects from foliage and fly-catches from perch. Nests near ground in dense, shrubby foliage.

Fairly common breeder late April–September, common migrant. Look for them at Saltese Flats, Crab Lake, Steptoe Butte SP, Bennington Lake, Toppenish NWR, Deschutes River State RA, John Day Fossil Beds NM, Leslie Gulch, Catlow Valley Road, Bullard Canyon, Fort Rock SP, and Putnam's Point.

Song a mix of whistles and burry notes. Call *tsiP*.

None in this realm.

ACCESSIBLE BIRDING SITES

State Parks

Each of the following parks includes accessible trails, but please contact individual parks for information regarding specific accommodations.

WASHINGTON

Bridgeport
Brooks Memorial
Columbia Plateau
Confluence State Park/
    Horan Natural Area
Crystal Falls
Curlew Lake
Daroga
Fields Spring
Fisk
Fort Simcoe
Ginkgo Petrified Forest
Ice Caves
Lake Lenore Caves
Lewis & Clark Trail
Lyons Ferry

Mount Spokane
Palouse to Cascades
Riverside
Sacajawea
Spokane River Centennial
Status Pass
Steamboat Rock
Steptoe Butte
Sun Lakes–Dry Falls

OREGON

Battle Mountain Forest
Catherine Creek
Collier Memorial
Cottonwood Canyon
Deschutes River State Recreation
    Area

Other Trails of Interest

Crooked River Wetlands Complex
Dishman Natural Area: Camp Caro
    Community Park and Trailhead
Turnbull National Wildlife Refuge

RECOMMENDED RESOURCES

Site Guides

A Birder's Guide to Washington,
wabirdguide.org

Birdability, birdability.org

Birds Connect Seattle Birding Sites,
birdweb.org

East Cascades Bird Alliance,
ecbirds.org/oregon-bird-
ing-guide/

Great Washington State Birding Trail,
wa.audubon.org/birds/great-
washington-state-birding-trail

Maps of Washington state birding
sites, wos.org/birding-resources/
maps/

Washington Birder County Check-
lists, wabirder.com

Washington Birder's Dashboard,
birddash.net/us/wa/

Real-Time Migration Information

Birdcast, birdcast.info

Bird Migration Explorer,
explorer.audubon.org

Birding by Ear

Birding by Ear,
audubon.org/birding-by-ear

Merlin Bird ID app by The Cornell
Lab of Ornithology

*Peterson Field Guide to Bird Sounds of
Western North America* by Nathan
Pieplow

Sibley Birds V2 app,
mydigitalearth.com

Comprehensive Field Guides

*National Geographic Field Guide to
the Birds of North America* by Jon-
athan Alderfer and Jon L. Dunn

The Sibley Guide to Birds by David
Allen Sibley

Regional Birding and Conservation Organizations

WASHINGTON

Audubon Washington,
wa.audubon.org

Birds Connect Seattle,
birdsconnectsea.org

Blue Mountain Audubon Society,
blumtn.org

Central Basin Audubon Society,
centralbasinaudubonsociety.org

Lower Columbia Basin Audubon
Society, lowercolumbiabasin-
audubon.org

North Central Washington Audubon
Society, ncwaudubon.org

Spokane Audubon Society,
audubonspokane.org

Washington Conservation Action
Education Fund, wecprotects.org

Washington Ornithological Society,
wos.org

Yakima Valley Audubon Society, yakimaaudubon.org

OREGON

Bird Alliance of Oregon, birdallianceoregon.org

East Cascades Bird Alliance, ecbirds.org

Klamath Basin Audubon Society, klamathaudubon.org

Klamath Bird Observatory, klamathbird.org

Oregon Birding Association, oregonbirding.org

Oregon Natural Desert Association, onda.org

Pendleton Bird Club, pendletonbirders.wordpress.com

Prineville Bird Club (private Facebook group)

National Birding and Conservation Organizations

American Bird Conservancy abcbirds.org

American Birding Association aba.org

Avian Knowledge Northwest avianknowledgenorthwest.net

National Audubon Society audubon.org

Urban Raptor Conservancy urbanraptorconservancy.org

Helping Birds

The Center for Environmental Law and Policy, celp.org

Energy Saver, energy.gov/energysaver/energy-saver

Pollution Prevention Tips for Water Conservation, epa.gov/p2/pollution-prevention-tips-water-conservation

"Twelve Tips to Help Migratory Birds on Their Way," abcbirds.org/ten-tips-spring-migration/

"Why Leashing Dogs Is an Easy Way to Protect Birds and Their Chicks," audubon.org/news/why-leashing-dogs-easy-way-protect-birds-and-their-chicks

ACKNOWLEDGMENTS

Those who say writing is a solitary act must not write. The publisher's team alone is a vast array of people, many of whom I will never know. Everyone I have worked with at Timber Press has been unfailingly pleasant, helpful, and kind, and for that, I am grateful.

Greg Smith has been a joy to work with. Not only did he take the hundreds of photos that grace this book, he also sourced images for the few birds he couldn't track down in the wild. Offering the answer to all identification conundrums, he kept track of the things that I lost sight of and provided valuable feedback on the manuscript.

Special thanks to Dr. Bruce, always, for comments and feedback and for fact-checking my assumptions. He and Professor Gullion, dear friends for decades, were also gracious enough to host me for the 2024 total solar eclipse. A sight to behold in the far Northeast Kingdom.

I am also grateful for Jacqueline, Lisa, Katie, and Thad, the writing group that keeps me moving. Our monthly meetings are invigorating and inspiring. I laugh as much as I learn.

There are, of course, many others for whom I am grateful, even if unnamed here.

Most importantly, those who dedicate their lives to making the world a better place in which to be a bird or nonhuman animal deserve recognition, gratitude, and unending support. Often unseen, usually significantly underpaid, and regularly lambasted for putting animals above humans, these are the people who work to keep a bit of wild among the human sprawl. May your field days be kind and your office days short. Thank you.

PHOTO AND ILLUSTRATION CREDITS

Public Domain
Lisa Hupp/USFWS, 244 (Adult Bohemian Waxwing)

Creative Commons Attribution 2.0 Generic
Amado Demesa, 210 (Adult Cassin's Vireo)

Andy Reago & Chrissy McClarren, 206 (Adult Chestnut-backed Chickadee)

Cephas, edit by Simonizer, 300 (Female Pine Grosbeak)

Frank Vassen, 254 (Juvenile)

Ron Knight, 300 (Male Pine Grosbeak)

USFWS Mountain-Prairie, 90 (Barrow's Goldeneye Male)

Creative Commons CC0 1.0 Universal Public Domain Dedication
Adam Jackson, 198 (Vaux's Swift Adult)

Creative Commons Attribution-Share Alike 3.0 Unported
Annette Teng, 198 (middle)

Cephus, 206 (Adult Black-capped Chickadee)

Richard Crossley, 198 (Adult White-throated Swift)

Creative Commons Attribution-Share Alike 4.0 International
Charles J. Sharp, 104 (Female), 202 (Adult Bank Swallows)

jakeschneider00, 164 (Adult Common Poorwill)

Mykola Swarnyk, 300 (Male and Female Evening Grosbeak)

Rhododendrites, 174 (Female Downy Woodpecker), 70 (Female)

Vickie J Anderson, www.wildlifeimagesupclose.com, 208 (Male Golden-crowned Kinglet), 238

VJAnderson, 226 (Adult Pacific Wren)

Family Silhouettes
Geese, Swans & Ducks by Kristtaps/iStock.com

Coots by iDrawSilhouettes/creativefabrica.com

Quail by sceneit/Vecteezy.com

Turkey by Save nature and wildlife/shutterstock.com

Grebes by Birchside/gograph.com

Cormorants by piranjya/iStock.com

Pelican from pngitem.com

Cranes by ArtistMiki/
shutterstock.com
Herons by Taras Adamovych/
Dreamstime.com
Plovers by Birchside/gograph.com
Sandpipers & Allies by Birchside/
gograph.com
Gulls & Terns by Birchside/
gograph.com
Vultures by iDrawSilhouettes/
creativefabrica.com
Osprey by UfimtsevaV/iStock.com
Hawks & Eagles by vadimmmus/
iStock.com
Falcons by PetrP/shutterstock.com
Pigeons & Doves by DeCe_X/
iStock.com
Owls by thesilhouettequeen/
123rf.com
Goatsuckers based on a photo by
Greg Smith
Kingfishers by Birchside/
gograph.com
Woodpeckers from pinclipart.com
Jays & Crows by Vector SpMan/
shutterstock.com
Hummingbirds by mr.Timmi/
shutterstock.com
Larks by Mrehssani/Dreamstime.com
Swifts by pngwing.com
Swallows by Ivana Kontic/
shutterstock.com
Chickadees by SilhouetteGarden.com
Kinglets based on an illustration
by Viktoria Karpunina/
shutterstock.com

Vireos based on a photo by
VJAnderson / Wiki-media Com-
mons (used under a CCA-SA 4.0
International license)
Flycatchers by Bahau/
shutterstock.com
Shrikes by Vitaly Ilyasov/
shutterstock.com
Wrens by Loveleen/stock.adobe.com
Dippers by Eric Carlson
Starlings by Bob Comix
Thrushes by Jackie/cleanpng.com
Waxwings by Bob Comix/creazilla.
com (used under a CCA 4.0
license)
Thrashers by Melinda Fawver/
shutterstock.com
Nuthatches / Creepers by wectors/
123rf.com
Creepers by Clker-free-vector-images
Finches by Stefanie Schubbert/
shutterstock.com
Sparrows by Noah Strycker/
shutterstock.com
Chats by Design_Stock7/
shutterstock.com
Blackbirds & Allies by Birchside/
gograph.com
Warblers by thesilhouettequeen/
123rf.com
Grosbeaks, Tanagers & Allies based
on a photo by Michael Fish

American Bird Conservancy. 2022. EPA signals continued use of insecticides dangerous to birds. 15 March 2022. https://abcbirds.org/news/epa-malathion-neonicotinoid-insecticide-opinion/

Billerman, S. M., B. K. Keeney, P. G. Rodewald, and T. S. Schulenberg, eds. 2020. Birds of the World (website). Ithaca, New York: Cornell Laboratory of Ornithology. birdsoftheworld.org/bow/home.

Cascades Volcano Observatory. 2023. Columbia River Basalt Group Stretches from Oregon to Idaho. US Geological Society (USGS).

Chesser, R. T., S. M. Billerman, K. J. Burns, C. Cicero, J. L. Dunn, B. E. Hernández-Baños, R. A. Jiménez, A. W. Kratter, N. A. Mason, P. C. Rasmussen, J. V. Remsen Jr., D. F. Stotz, and K. Winker. 2022. Checklist of North and Middle American Birds. American Ornithological Society. https://checklist.americanornithology.org/taxa

Cullinan, T. 2001. *Important Bird Areas of Washington*. Olympia: Washington Audubon. https://wa.audubon.org/conservation/important-bird-areas-washington

Dubey, A., M. T. Lewis, G. P. Dively, and K. A. Hamly. Ecological impacts of pesticide seed treatments on arthropod communities in a grain crop rotation. *Journal of Applied Ecology*, vol. 57, 21 Feb. 2020, pp. 936–951, https://besjournals.onlinelibrary.wiley.com/doi/full/10.1111/1365-2664.13595

Female Bird Day. https://femalebirdday.wordpress.com

Frank, S. D., and J. F. Tooker. 2020. Neonicotinoids pose undocumented threats to food webs. *Proceedings of the National Academy of Sciences*. 117(37): 22609–22613. https://doi.org/10.1073/pnas.2017221117

International Union for Conservation of Nature and Natural Resources (IUCN). The IUCN Red List of Threatened Species. https://www.iucnredlist.org/

Irons, D. 2018. *American Birding Association Field Guide to Birds of Oregon*. New York: Scott and Nix, Inc.

Johnson, C. G. Jr. 2004. *Alpine and Subalpine Vegetation of the Wallowa, Seven Devils, and Blue Mountains*. US Department of Agriculture, Forest Service. https://www.fs.usda.gov/Internet/FSE_DOCUMENTS/fseprd1178128.pdf

McClure, D. 2016. Shrub Steppe: The forgotten ecosystem of eastern Washington. https://palouseaudubon.org/wp-content/uploads/2016/09/shrbstpfrgteco.pdf

Ohio-Kentucky-Indiana Water Science Center. 2017. Pesticides. US Geological Survey. https://www.usgs.gov/centers/ohio-kentucky-indiana-water-science-center/science/pesticides

Oregon Department of Fish and Wildlife. The Oregon conservation strategy 2016. https://www.oregonconservationstrategy.org/overview/

Partners in Flight. 2024. Avian conservation assessment database. Bird Conservancy of the Rockies. https://pif.birdconservancy.org/avian-conservation-assessment-database/

Paulson, D. 2020. *American Birding Association Field Guide to Birds of Washington*. New York: Scott and Nix, Inc.

Rakestraw, J. 2023. *Birding Oregon: A Guide to the Best Birding Sites across the State*. Third edition. Self-published.

Seattle Audubon Society. 2022. BirdWeb: Seattle Audubon's Guide to the Birds of Washington. https://birdweb.org/birdweb/

Shewey, J., and T. Blount. 2017. *Birds of the Pacific Northwest*. Portland, Oregon: Timber Press.

Sibley, D. A. 2002. *Sibley's Birding Basics: How to Identify Birds, Using the Clues in Feathers, Habitats, Behaviors, and Sounds*. New York: Alfred A. Knopf.

Sibley, D. A. 2016. *The Sibley Field Guide to Birds of Western North America*. New York: Alfred A. Knopf.

Stewart, R. E. 2016. Technical aspects of wetlands as bird habitat. *National Water Summary on Wetland Resources*. https://water.usgs.gov/nwsum/WSP2425/birdhabitat.html

Taylor, R. J. 2003. *Sagebrush Country: A Wildflower Sanctuary*. Missoula, Montana: Mountain Press Publishing Company.

Thomas, R. 2011. Nature notes: bird flight over water. Loyola University, New Orleans. https://lucec.loyno.edu/natural-history-writings/bird-flight-over-water

US Environmental Protection Agency. 2022. *Wetlands*. Updated August 23, 2022. https://www.epa.gov/wetlands

Washington Department of Fish & Wildlife. 2008. Priority habitat and species list. Olympia, Washington.

Washington Department of Fish & Wildlife. 2015. Washington's state wildlife action plan 2015 update. https://wdfw.wa.gov/species-habitats/at-risk/swap

Washington Department of Fish & Wildlife. 2022. Ecosystems in Washington. https://wdfw.wa.gov/species-habitats/ecosystems/

Washington Ornithological Society. 2015. *A Birder's Guide to Washington* (second edition), J. Hadley (ed.). Delaware City, DE: American Birding Association.

Weidensaul, S. 2022. Neonic nation: Is widespread pesticide use connected to grassland bird declines? https://www.allaboutbirds.org/news/neonic-nation-is-widespread-pesticide-use-connected-to-grassland-bird-declines/

Weis, P., and W. Newman. 2006. *The Channeled Scablands of Eastern Washington: The Geologic Story of the Spokane Flood.* https://www.nps.gov/parkhistory/online_books/geology/publications/inf/72-2/contents.htm

Photo by Lou Schwarz

About the Author

TAMARA ENZ is a writer, photographer, and biologist. Watching swirling Barn Swallows, being awakened by the summer breeding-frenzied cacophony, and seeing the tiniest birds fluff into balls of winter warmth captured her from the beginning. After studying birds in habitats as varied as the Arctic Ocean and the New Mexico desert, she is no less fascinated by their antics and no less envious of their ability to fly. Tamara lives wherever she is. You can find her, and *her* antics, at The Road not Taken Enough, TamaraEnz.com.

Photo by Lou Schwarz

About the Photographer

GREGORY "SLOBIRDR" SMITH is a biologist and an itinerant photographer and natural history guide. He bought his first SLR at age twelve and has been chasing the elusive "perfect" photo of many of the world's bird species ever since. Having made a goal of traveling the continents over the years, he has found himself in some unique photographic situations, which you can witness at Flickr.com/photos/slobirdr.